REREADING LITERATURE
William Shakespeare

William Shakespeare

Terry Eagleton

Basil Blackwell

© Terry Eagleton 1986

First published 1986

Basil Blackwell Ltd
108 Cowley Road, Oxford OX4 1JF, UK

Basil Blackwell Inc.
432 Park Avenue South, Suite 1505,
New York, NY 10016, USA

British Library Cataloguing in Publication Data

Eagleton, Terry
  William Shakespeare.—(Rereading literature)
  1. Shakespeare, William—Criticism and
  interpretation
  I. Title   II. Series
  822'.3'3   PR2976

  ISBN 0–631–14553–2
  ISBN 0–631–14554–0 Pbk

Library of Congress Cataloging in Publication Data

Eagleton, Terry, 1943–
  William Shakespeare.

  (Rereading literature)
  Includes index.
  1. Shakespeare, William, 1564–1616—Criticism and interpretation.
I. Title.   II. Series: Re-reading literature.
PR2976.E17 1986   822.3'3   85–22927
ISBN 0–631–14553–2
ISBN 0–631–14554–0 (pbk.)

Typeset by Cambrian Typesetters, Frimley, Surrey
Printed in Great Britain by Billing & Sons Ltd, Worcester

For Anne and Mary

Contents

Preface

The Monty Python team once presented a 'Summarize Proust' contest, in which competitors were given twenty seconds to summarize the plot of Proust's novel, first in bathing costume and then in evening dress. The present project seems only slightly less foolhardy. I have made no attempt to deal with the whole of Shakepeare's work, though I have written, however briefly, about most of what are generally agreed to be the major plays. This is done with only rough respect for chronology and no particular attention to generic divisions, the importance of which seems to me overrated. On the whole I have written about the plays which interest me, with the aim of developing a particular case about Shakespearian drama, one centred on the interrelations of language, desire, law, money and the body, which can be taken further into Shakespeare's work by anybody concerned to do so. The book is in no direct sense an historical study of its topic, but is, I suppose, an exercise in political semiotics, which tries to locate the relevant history in the very letter of the text.

Those who are sceptical of the relevance of contemporary critical theory to the Swan of Avon should remember that there are more anachronisms in Shakespeare's plays than the clock in *Julius Caesar*. Though conclusive evidence is hard to come by, it is difficult to read Shakespeare without feeling that he was almost certainly familiar with the writings of Hegel, Marx, Nietzsche, Freud, Wittgenstein and Derrida. Perhaps this is simply to say that though there are many ways in which we have thankfully left this conservative patriarch behind, there are other ways in which we have yet to catch up with him.

I am very grateful to my English colleagues at Wadham College, Robin Robbins and Alan Ward, for sharing with me their scholarly expertise on a number of points, though neither can be accused of complicity with my arguments. I would also like to thank Catherine Belsey, John Carey, Philip Carpenter, Jonathan Dollimore, Emrys Jones and David Norbrook for their generous help and advice in the preparation of this book. All quotations from Shakespeare are taken from Peter Alexander (ed.), *William Shakespeare: The Complete Works* (London and Glasgow, 1962).

Terry Eagleton

1 Language: *Macbeth, Richard II, Henry IV*

I

Even those who know very little about Shakespeare might be vaguely aware that his plays value social order and stability, and that they are written with an extraordinary eloquence, one metaphor breeding another in an apparently unstaunchable flow of what modern theorists might call 'textual productivity'. The problem is that these two aspects of Shakespeare are in potential conflict with one another. For a stability of signs – each word securely in place, each signifier (mark or sound) corresponding to its signified (or meaning) – is an integral part of any social order: settled meanings, shared definitions and regularities of grammar both reflect, and help to constitute, a well-ordered political state. Yet it is all this which Shakespeare's flamboyant punning, troping and riddling threaten to put into question. His belief in social stability is jeopardized by the very language in which it is articulated. It would seem, then, that the very act of writing implies for Shakespeare an epistemology (or theory of knowledge) at odds with his political ideology. This is a deeply embarrassing dilemma, and it is not surprising that much of Shakespeare's drama is devoted to figuring out strategies for resolving it.

To any unprejudiced reader – which would seem to

exclude Shakespeare himself, his contemporary audiences and almost all literary critics – it is surely clear that positive value in *Macbeth* lies with the three witches. The witches are the heroines of the piece, however little the play itself recognizes the fact, and however much the critics may have set out to defame them. It is they who, by releasing ambitious thoughts in Macbeth, expose a reverence for hierarchial social order for what it is, as the pious self-deception of a society based on routine oppression and incessant warfare. The witches are exiles from that violent order, inhabiting their own sisterly community on its shadowy borderlands, refusing all truck with its tribal bickerings and military honours. It is their riddling, ambiguous speech (they 'palter with us in a double sense') which promises to subvert this structure: their teasing word-play infiltrates and undermines Macbeth from within, revealing in him a lack which hollows his being into desire. The witches signify a realm of non-meaning and poetic play which hovers at the work's margins, one which has its own kind of truth; and their words to Macbeth catalyse this region of otherness and desire within himself, so that by the end of the play it has flooded up from within him to shatter and engulf his previously assured identity. In this sense the witches figure as the 'unconscious' of the drama, that which must be exiled and repressed as dangerous but which is always likely to return with a vengeance. That unconscious is a discourse in which meaning falters and slides, in which firm definitions are dissolved and binary oppositions eroded: fair is foul and foul is fair, nothing is but what is not. Androgynous (bearded women), multiple (three-in-one) and 'imperfect speakers', the witches strike at the stable social, sexual and linguistic forms which the society of the play needs in order to survive. They perform a 'deed without a name', and Macbeth's own actions, once influenced by them, become such that 'Tongue nor heart/ Cannot conceive nor name'. The physical fluidity of the three sisters becomes inscribed in Macbeth's own restless desire, continually pursuing the pure being of kingship but at each step ironically unravelling that very possibility: 'To be thus is nothing,/But to be safely thus.' Macbeth ends up chasing an identity which continually eludes him; he becomes a floating signifier in ceaseless, doomed pursuit of an anchoring signified:

> Life's but a walking shadow, a poor player,
> That struts and frets his hour upon the stage,
> And then is heard no more; it is a tale
> Told by an idiot, full of sound and fury,
> Signifying nothing.
>
> (V.v.24–8)

He is reduced to a ham actor, unable to identify with his role.

As the most fertile force in the play, the witches inhabit an anarchic, richly ambiguous zone both in and out of official society: they live in their own world but intersect with Macbeth's. They are poets, prophetesses and devotees of female cult, radical separatists who scorn male power and lay bare the hollow sound and fury at its heart. Their words and bodies mock rigorous boundaries and make sport of fixed positions, unhinging received meanings as they dance, dissolve and re-materialize. But official society can only ever imagine its radical 'other' as chaos rather than creativity, and is thus bound to define the sisters as evil. Foulness – a political order which thrives on bloodshed – believes itself fair, whereas the witches do not so much invert this opposition as deconstruct it. Macbeth himself fears the troubling of exact definitions: to be authentically human is, in his view, to be creatively constrained, fixed and framed by certain precise bonds of hierarchical allegiance. Beyond these lies the dissolute darkness of the witches into which, by murdering Duncan, he will catapult himself at a stroke. To transgress these determining bonds, for Macbeth, is to become less than human in trying to become more, a mere self-cancelling liberty:

> I dare do all that may become a man;
> Who dares do more is none.
>
> (I.vii.46–7)

Too much inverts itself into nothing at all. Later Ross will speak of 'float[ing] upon a wild and violent sea,/Each way and none', meaning that to move in all directions at once is to stand still.

Lady Macbeth holds the opposite view: transgression, the ceaseless surpassing of limits, is for her the very mark of the human:

> When you durst do it, then you were a man;
> And to be more than what you were, you would
> Be so much more the man.
>
> (I.vii.49–51)

She herself crosses the strict divide of gender roles and cries out to be unsexed, flouting Angelo's paternalistic advice to Isabella in *Measure for Measure*:

> Be that you are,
> That is, a woman; if you be more, you're none. . .
>
> (II,iv.134–5)

Like most of Shakespeare's villains, in short, Lady Macbeth is a bourgeois individualist, for whom traditional ties of rank and kinship are less constitutive of personal identity than mere obstacles to be surmounted in the pursuit of one's private ends. But the witches are hardly to be blamed for this, whatever Macbeth's own jaundiced view of the matter. For one thing they live in community, not as individual entrepreneurs of the self; and unlike the Macbeths they are indifferent to political power because they have no truck with linear time, which is always, so to speak, on the side of Caesar.

The Macbeths' impulse to transgress inhabits history: it is an endless expansion of the self in a single trajectory, an unslakable thirst for some ultimate mastery which will never come. The witches' subversiveness moves within cyclical time, centred on dance, the moon, pre-vision and verbal repetition, inimical to linear history and its imperial themes of sexual reproduction.[1] It is such lineage – the question of which particular male will inherit political power – which they garble and confound in their address to Macbeth and Banquo, as well as in their most lethal piece of double-talk of all: 'none of woman born shall harm Macbeth'. Like the unconscious, the witches know no narrative; but once the creative dissolution they signify is inflected *within* the political system, it can always take the form of a 'freedom' which remains enslaved to the imperatives of power, a desire which merely reproduces, sexually and politically, the same old story and the same oppressive law. There is a style of transgression which is play and poetic non-sense, a dark carnival in which all formal values are satirized and deranged;[2] and there is the different but related disruptiveness of bourgeois individualist appetite, which, in its ruthless drive to be all, sunders every constraint and lapses back into nothing. Such ambition is as self-undoing as the porter's drink, provoking desire but taking away the performance: unlike the fruitful darkness of the witches, it is a nothing from which nothing can come.

This ambivalence of transgression is well captured in the *Communist Manifesto*. The bourgeoisie, Marx and Engels write, cannot exist without constantly revolutionizing all social relations:

> Constant revolutionizing of production, uninterrupted disturbance of all social conditions, everlasting uncertainty and agitation distinguish the bourgeois epoch from all earlier ones. All fixed, fast-frozen relations, with their train of ancient and venerable prejudices and opinions, are swept away, all newformed ones become antiquated before they can ossify. All that is solid melts into air, all that is holy is profaned, and man is at last compelled to face with sober senses his real conditions of life, and his relations with his kind.[3]

'All that is solid melts into air, all that is holy is profaned': this is the positive trespassing and travestying of the witches, who dissolve into thin air and disfigure all sacred values. Yet this liquidation of all 'fixed, fast-frozen relations' is, in the case of the bourgeoisie, finally self-destructive, breeding new forms of exploitation which in the end will undo it. Like Macbeth, the bourgeoisie will become entangled in its own excess, giving birth to its own gravedigger (the working class), dissolving away that obstacle to historical development which is itself, and dying of its own too much. The universal wolf of appetite, as Ulysses remarks in *Troilus and Cressida*, 'Must make perforce an universal prey,/And last eat up himself' (I.iii.123–4). Lady Macbeth is akin to the three sisters in celebrating female power, but in modern parlance she is a 'bourgeois' feminist who strives to outdo in domination and virility the very male system which subordinates her. Even so, it is hard to see why her bloodthirsty talk of dashing out babies' brains is any more 'unnatural' than skewering an enemy soldier's guts. Meek women, military carnage and aristocratic titles are supposed by the play to be natural; witches and regicide are not. Yet this opposition will not hold even within *Macbeth*'s own terms, since the 'unnatural' – Macbeth's lust for power – is disclosed by the witches as already lurking within the 'natural' – the routine state of cut-throat rivalry between noblemen. Nature harbours the unnatural within its bosom, and does so as one of its conditions of being: since Nature can be defined only by reference to its so-called perversions, Macbeth is right to believe that nothing is but what is not. Nature, to be normative, must already include the possibility of its own perversion, just as a sign can be roughly defined as anything which can be used for the purpose of lying.[4] A mark which did not structurally contain the capacity to be abused would not be called a sign. The fact that Macbeth's conqueror was born by caesarean section (that is, 'unnaturally') is an 'unnatural', patriarchal repression of men's dependency on women; but the witches do well to steer clear of sexual reproduction in a society where birth determines whom you may 'naturally' exploit, dispossess or defer to.

In killing Duncan, symbol of the body politic, Macbeth is, in the play's ideological terms, striking at the physical root of his own life, so that the act of regicide is also a form of bodily self-estrangement. In a graphic gesture of self-division, his hand will try to clutch a dagger bred by his own brain. Language – the equivocal enigmas of the witches – overwhelms and dismembers the body; desire inflates consciousness to the point where it dissevers itself from sensuous constraints and comes to consume itself in a void. When language is cut loose from reality, signifiers split from signifieds, the result is a radical fissure between consciousness and material life. Macbeth will end up as a bundle of broken signifiers, his body reduced to a blind automaton of battle; his sleepwalking wife disintegrates into fragments of hallucinated speech and mindless physical action. Duncan's commendation of the bleeding sergeant ('So well thy words become thee as thy wounds') suggests, by contrast, an organic unity of body and speech. The body is a duplicitous signifier, sometimes transparently expressive of an inner essence, sometimes, as with Macbeth's countenance, a cryptic text to be deciphered. As we shall see throughout this study, Shakespeare feels the need to integrate a potentially overweening conciousness within the body's sure limits, a process which is for him inseparable from the integration of individuals into the body politic. It also involves a restabilizing of the sign, restoring floating signifiers to their appropriate signifieds, for meaning is the 'spirit' of words which should find true incarnation in their material forms. The problem is how to do all this without suppressing what is productive about individual energies, and suggestive about the sliding, metaphorical word.

The Macbeths are finally torn apart in the contradiction between body and language, between the frozen bonds of traditional allegiance and the unassuageable dynamic of desire. The witches experience no such conflict because their very bodies are not static but mutable, melting as breath into the wind, ambivalently material and im-material, and so, as 'breath' suggests, with all the protean quality of language itself. One exit-route from the tragedy of the play, in short, would be to have a different sort of body altogether, one which had escaped from singular identity into diffusion and plurality. Shakespeare will return to this idea in his very last drama in the figure of Ariel. But *Macbeth* fears this feminine fluidity as political anarchy, viewing diffusion as disruption. One of its more creditable reasons for doing so, as we shall see later, is that it is worried by the closeness of this fruitful interchangeability of signs, roles and bodies to a certain destructive tendency in bourgeois thought which levels all differences to the same dead level, in the anarchy and arbitrariness of the market-place.[5]

II

When signs detach themselves from the material world, a curious paradox tends to result. On the one hand, such signs are now purely vacuous, dead letters emptied of all constraining content and so free to couple promiscuously with each other in an orgy of inbreeding. On the other hand, signs which have shaken themselves loose from the world now stand at an *operative* distance from it, able to reach back into reality and mould it to their own capricious designs. Shakespeare is continually struck at once by the 'nothing' of such estranged language, its lack of ground or substance, and its power to bend the world to its own will. The sign as fetish, shorn of a significant context to become an end in itself, is ironically the sign at its most materially potent, manipulating real situations until it and they seem once more inextricable. When this discourse is that of a tyrannical monarch, this particular paradox unites with another. For the king is at once impersonal symbol of the social order, expressive of its corporate meanings, yet able in his arbitrary decrees to stand free of that order and dominate it from the outside. His word is 'creative': discourse, not least royal discourse, is material power, an active intervention into the world at least as real as a blow on the head. Yet this creativity is uneasily close to a kind of discursive imperialism, in which words determine reality rather than the other way round.

Something like this seems to happen in *Richard II*. The play opens with a linguistic impasse: Bolingbroke and Mowbray accuse each other of treason in ritualized, rhetorical form, and since the issue remains verbally unresolvable it can be decided only by an appeal to the body. The two men will try to kill each other to prove their point. 'What I speak', declares Bolingbroke, 'My body shall make good upon this earth': actions will authenticate signs, flushing them with authentic physical content. When Richard sentences Bolingbroke to exile he robs him of his native speech, rips 'breath' or language from his body, and thus leaves it a kind of inexpressive corpse:

> The language I have learnt these forty years,
> My native English, now I must forgo;
> And now my tongue's use is to me no more
> Than an unstringed viol or a harp. . .
> Within my mouth you have engaol'd my tongue,
> Doubly portcullis'd with my teeth and lips. . .
> (I.iii.159–64)

To be banished from the air of one's native land is to be drained of the breath of its language; in exiling Bolingbroke Richard has dissevered his body and language as effectively as death would disjoin them. Whimsically relenting, Richard then curtails Bolingbroke's sentence by four years, refashioning reality by his word as surely as one might transform it by action:

> How long a time lies in one little word!
> Four lagging winters and four wanton springs
> End in a word: such is the breath of Kings.
> (I.iii.213–15)

Language is not, however, as all-powerful as Richard's word makes it sound: it hovers on some indeterminate borderline between nullity and omnipotence. When Gaunt tries to temper Bolingbroke's dejection by persuading him to imagine his banishment as pleasurable, his son brusquely rejects this glib appeal to metaphor:

O, who can hold a fire in his hand
By thinking on the frosty Caucasus?
Or cloy the hungry edge of appetite
By bare imagination of a feast?
Or wallow naked in December snow
By thinking on fantastic summer's heat?

(I.iii.294–9)

There is a recalcitrance about the material world which trope and fiction cannot dissolve, a material limit before which the power of discourse is disarmed. Aumerle comments tartly a little later that had the word 'farewell' added years to Bolingbroke's exile he would have given him a volume of them, 'But since it would not, he had none from me'.

When the dying Gaunt puns on his own name, Richard finds this word-play profoundly irritating: 'Can sick men play so nicely with their names?' This is pretty rich, coming as it does from a king who seems unable to scratch his nose without making a symbol out of it. As a 'poet king', Richard trusts to the sway of the signifier: only by translating unpleasant political realities into decorative verbal fictions can he engage with them. While Bolingbroke's armies are invading, Richard wants to sit down and concoct narcissistic narratives about the death of kings. He survives his deposition only by rewriting it as a tragic drama, and when brought finally to execution can face death only by cobbling together a brief Metaphysical poem on the topic. Such portentous myth-making is quite at one with his ruthless political opportunism. When symbolism drifts free of political reality to become an end in itself, it leaves that reality drained of significant value and so as mere brute material to be pragmatically exploited. It is not surprising that Richard, like so many modern politicians, is both

callous and sentimental. But the signifier has divorced itself
from society only to reorganize it according to its own laws.
Richard has mortgaged the realm of England, so that the
whole country is now 'leas'd out', held together with 'inky
blots and rotten parchment bonds'. The social order is
stitched together by empty words, patched up by financial
discourse, which itself stands in for money, and that in turn
stands in for material labour. Textual fictions determine
the economic life of England, just as the king's self-
regarding rhetoric dominates its politics: Richard wonders
at one point whether his 'word be sterling yet in England'.
Gaunt, by contrast, practises economy in his speech,
backing each deathbed word to Richard with the physical
labour and moral authority of his dying, and thus
countering the king's own debasement of verbal currency:

> Where words are scarce, they are seldom spent in
> vain;
> For they breathe true that breathe their words in pain.
> He that no more must say is listen'd more
> Than they whom youth and ease have taught to
> glose. . .

> (II.i.7–10)

Little, in a state of linguistic inflation, becomes more, just
as all becomes nothing. Speaking too much means com-
municating less, whereas to say enough is to say everything.
(In *Henry IV, Part 1*, Henry describes the taste of sweetness
as a state in which 'a little/More than a little is by much too
much' (III.ii.); and in *As You Like It* Rosalind notes that
wine pours out of a narrow-necked bottle either too much at
once or none at all.) In Richard's England, relations
between signs have come to determine relations between
individuals and things: the king is a 'pelican' who sucks his
own life-blood like the self-parasitical word. Gaunt's
deathbed paltering seeks to undo this with a *creative*
deployment of metaphor, one which illuminates rather than
obscures real social conditions. To do this with as irascible
a king as Richard is clearly a delicate business: Gaunt's

tongue, Richard curtly reminds him, could 'run thy head from thy unreverent shoulders', his own expiring breath succeed in decapitating him. Discourse kills as well as creates: York later points out to Northumberland, who has omitted the king's title in conversation, that:

> The time hath been,
> Would you have been so brief with him, he would
> Have been so brief with you to shorten you,
> For taking so the head, your whole head's length.
>
> (III.iii.12–15)

As Richard's gorgeous symbolism, the title, rhetoric and insignia of kingship, slowly disintegrates before the laconic Bolingbroke, so his identity comes gradually apart at the seams:

> . . . I have no name, no title –
> No, not that name was given me at the font –
> But 'tis usurp'd. . . .
>
> (IV.i.255–7)

He is conseqently brought to death – in one sense the ultimate reality, in another sense the consummation of nothingness – and finds in it his most accomplished theatrical moment. Something comes of nothing, as Richard wrests his most elaborate fiction from the process of being dismantled.

How real is the signifier is a question which *Richard II* constantly poses. Language is something less than reality, but also its very inner form; and it is difficult to distinguish this 'proper' intertwining of signs and things, in which image and symbol are the very enabling grammar of human relations, from that 'improper' commingling of the two which springs from the imperial interventions of the autonomous sign, shaping reality to its self-indulgent whims. Myth and metaphor should service rather than master society; yet they are not purely supplementary to it either, mere disposable ornaments, since they shape from within the history to which they give outward expression.

Fiction seems inherent in reality: politics works by rhetoric and mythology, power is histrionic, and since social roles appear arbitrarily interchangeable, society itself is a dramatic artefact, demanding a certain suspension of disbelief on the part of its members. Macbeth has seen through it all by the time of his death, glimpsed the vacuous theatricality of life and the random nature of all identity in that night of the witches where all cats are black. There is no social reality without its admixture of feigning, mask, performance, delusion, just as there is no sign which cannot be used to deceive. Being yourself always involves a degree of play-acting, and the most deceived actor – the one who identifies entirely with his role – is the most convincing in reality.

Actors are, so to speak, signifiers who strive to become one with the signifieds of their parts; yet however successfully they achieve this we know that such representation is a lie, that the actor is not the character, and the stage is other than the world. The more an actor 'hollows out' his individual identity to unite with his role, the more authentic a performer he becomes. This for Shakespeare is true of all individuals, not just for actors. The more Macbeth nails himself to his allocated social function, suppressing whatever guilty desires might seek to transgress it, the more real a man he is. True identity thus thrives by repression, and genuine freedom lies in bondage. The self is nothing of what it is not: it survives by banishing those forces within it which threaten to usurp its sovereignty. But since bondage, to be authentic, must spring from free consent ('I am your free dependant', the Provost of *Measure for Measure* tells the Duke), that free act can always be turned against it. The self lives an irresolvable division between its desire, which conducts it along an endless chain of inflated signifiers, and its efforts at an 'imaginary' unity with the fixed signified of its social position.[6] As far as Hamlet is concerned, such efforts are hardly worth the trouble.

If representation is a lie, then the very structure of the

theatrical sign is strangely duplicitous, asserting an identity while manifesting a division, and to this extent it resembles the structure of metaphor. For metaphor works simultaneously by difference and identity, claiming that passion *is* fire, while undermining that claim in the same breath – for how can one thing be some other thing? Nothing is but what it is not, metaphor proposes; and while this sharpens our sense of a thing's unique qualities (we now know that passion is fiery), it also threatens to equalize differences into an endlessly repeated identity, a condition in which everything comes to mirror everything else. In this sense metaphor operates rather like money, which, as Timon of Athens protests in a passage quoted with relish by Marx, can convert any distinctive quality into any other:

> Thus much of this will make black white, foul fair,
> Wrong right, base noble, old young, coward valiant. . .
> This yellow slave
> Will knit and break religions, bless th'accurs'd,
> Make the hoar leprosy ador'd, place thieves
> And give them title, knee, and approbation,
> With senators on the bench. . .
>
> (IV.iii.28–34)

The *current* is what is new, and therefore, one would expect, different; but currency is also that which exchanges at the standard rates, and so a tedious repetition of the old familiar story. Similarly, metaphor promises fresh insight by its play of signs, disrupting the self-identity of things (passion is now fire), but achieves this new knowledge only at the price of 'exchanging' its two signs as equivalent values, foisting upon them a sameness which they resist. Money is nothing in itself: like language it derives value only from its use within material forms of life. Yet when it grows autonomous of that life, fetishized to a thing in itself, it becomes a kind of double nothing. It is now not only nothing in itself, but by sucking substance from the objects it is supposed to mediate strips them of their distinctive qualities and leaves them abstractly commutable. Its omnipotence, like Macbeth's ambition or Richard's kingly word, is a concealed form of impotence: by conflating all values ambiguously together it reduces them, and itself, to inert indifference. There is something hollow at the very heart of society, something rotten in the state, which is the very condition of its real existence.

If the self in Shakespeare is divided between desire and position, then characters who have scant regard for the latter are likely to escape a potentially tragic disunity. Sir John Falstaff of *Henry IV* is more at home with drunks than dukes, and so represents a danger to political stability apparent at once in his body and speech. His body is so grossly material that he can hardly move; his language so shifty that it resists all truth. Within the single figure of Falstaff, both body and language are pressed to a self-parodic extreme. He falls 'below' social order in being too sheerly, stubbornly himself, a brazen hedonist who refuses to conform the body's drives to social decorum. Yet he also falls 'beyond' that order in his fantastical speech, as hollow as his body is full, which can spin twelve rogues in buckram suits out of two in as many lines. Falstaff can turn the brute materiality of the body against the airy abstractions of ruling-class rhetoric:

> Can honour set a leg? No. Or an arm? No. Or take away the grief of a wound? No. Honour hath no skill in surgery, then? No. What is honour? A word. What is in that word? Honour. What is that honour? Air.
>
> (1.V.i.130–4)

But he is himself one of Shakespeare's most shameless verbal mystifiers, divorcing word from deed in his pathological boasting, recklessly erasing distinctions in his metaphorical excess:

> *Falstaff* ...'Sblood, I am as melancholy as a gib cat or a lugg'd bear.
> *Prince*   Or an old lion, or a lover's lute.

> Falstaff   Yea, or the drone of a Lincolnshire bagpipe.
> Prince   What sayest thou to a hare, or the melancholy
>   of Moor Ditch?
>
> (1.I.ii.71–6)

If Falstaff appeals to the sensuous facts of the body to
deflate ideological illusions, he also has a remarkably
cavalier way with such facts:

> Falstaff   Give me a cup of sack; I am a rogue if I
>   drunk today.
> Prince   O villain! thy lips are scarce wip'd since thou
>   drunk'st last.
> Falstaff   All is one for that.

Both aspects of Falstaff – reductive materialism and verbal
licence – belong to the carnivalesque, the satiric comedy of
the people; but it is interesting to note their incongruity.
Social order is subverted simultaneously from two opposed
directions: by that which is purely and materially itself, the
self-pleasuring body which refuses to be inscribed by social
imperatives; and by that which is never at one with itself at
all, the iconoclastic idiom of those who run verbal rings
round their solemnly prosaic opponents. Unlike the con-
summately self-conscious Henry and Hal, Falstaff is in one
sense an indifferent actor, playing only himself, at ease
within his own voluminous space and incapable of deferring
or dissembling his appetites; yet in the tavern drama he
shifts fluently between the parts of Hal and Henry, with the
infinite opportunism of one who is both all and nothing.

From this viewpoint, the character in *Henry IV, Part 1*
who most resembles Falstaff is, curiously, Hotspur. Hotspur
is, of course, a man of action; yet his fiery imagination tends
to overreach itself to the point where his rhetoric grows self-
generating, as in his exchanges with Worcester and
Northumberland in Act I, scene iii. Hal's words over his
corpse at the end of the play capture this disparity between
confining body and overriding spirit:

Ill-weav'd ambition, how much art thou shrunk!
When that this body did contain a spirit,
A kingdom for it was too small a bound;
But now two paces of the vilest earth
Is room enough.

(V.iv.88–92)

Hotspur parallels Falstaff also in his scornful opposition of
body to words; both man of action and man of inertia are
paradoxically akin in this. Hotspur refuses the King
prisoners because of the mincing accents of the 'popinjay'
who comes to demand them; he points to Mortimer's
wounds as 'mouths', adequately expressive without aid of
speech of the man's loyalty, and is mimicked by Hal as a
man whose language absurdly understates his military
prowess. He also resents Northumberland's sending letters
to the rebel camp rather than appearing in person, viewing
this as a cowardly substitution of textual for physical
presence. The difference between the two figures is that
Hotspur is an old-style idealist who desires a language
adequate to action and vice versa; Falstaff has not the
slightest wish to integrate the two, but flourishes in the gulf
between them. The organic unities of the traditional social
order, the solid word coupled to the speaking deed, are now
being splintered apart, as language flies off into non-
meaning and the body sinks steadily into grossness. *Henry
IV, Part 2* will open with the figure of Rumour, a wild
polyphony of prattling half-truths, and close with a
deceiving pun: Jerusalem, where prophecy assured Henry
he would die, turns out to be a bedchamber in his palace.
The ambiguous signifier, for Henry as for Macbeth, robs
you of any final resting place.

2 Desire: *A Midsummer Night's Dream, Twelfth Night*

I

The place where language and the body most obviously intersect is in sexual desire. For if sexual desire is a physical matter, it is even more (as Shakespeare well appreciates) a question of discourse: sonnets, love letters, verbal fencing, seductive rhetoric. Indeed the disproportion between these two aspects of sexuality in Shakespeare is striking: the elaborate idioms of desire – lovers' quarrels, courting rituals, moonstruck maunderings – are all 'about' the physical act of coition itself, yet seem absurdly excessive of it, to the point where one begins to wonder whether the truth is not the reverse, and the physical act merely provides a convenient occasion for certain forms of verbal display. Since the sexual act itself cannot be performed on stage, its absence from the language which surrounds it is all the more eloquent. But it is not clear whether physical sex is the missing 'real' – off-stage, so to speak – which would finally ground all this baroque rhetoric in something definite, or whether it is merely incidental to the poetry itself, a trivial, well-nigh dispensable supplement to it.

Shakespearian comedy is acutely aware that characters in love are simultaneously at their most 'real' and 'unreal', most true and most feigning. Love is the ultimate self-definition, the most precious and unique mode of being; yet it is also intolerably hackneyed and banal, something that millions of people have done before and millions more will do again. To say 'I love you', as Jonathan Culler points out, is always at some level a quotation;[1] in its very moment of absolute, original value, the self stumbles across nothing but other people's lines, finds itself handed a meticulously detailed script to which it must slavishly conform. It discovers, that is, that it is always already 'written', scored through in its noblest thoughts and most spontaneous affections by the whole tediously repetitive history of human sexual behaviour, subjected to impersonal codes and conventions at exactly the moment it feels most euphorically free of them. Sexuality is a theatre with a strictly limited array of roles: cold mistress, unrequited lover, jealous paranoiac, unblemished madonna, vampiric whore. The most 'natural' human activity is thus a question of high artifice, as is perhaps most obvious when Shakespearian characters *write* their love to each other, deploying stilted literary formulae to articulate that which supposedly beggars all description. *Love's Labour's Lost* is much preoccupied with such ironic discrepancies between high-falutin poetic discourse and the plain impulses of sexual attraction. Language, once touched by such desire, tends to run riot: as Benedick remarks of the love-struck Claudio in *Much Ado About Nothing*, 'He was wont to speak plain and to the purpose, like an honest man and a soldier, and now he is turned orthography; his words are a very fantastical banquet, just so many strange dishes' (II.iii). The love between Benedick and Beatrice in *Much Ado* is the effect of elaborately fictitious information fed to each partner, so that it is impossible to decide whether this groundless discourse uncovers a love which was 'naturally' there, or actually constructs it. The mordant, sardonic wit of this admirable pair of iconoclasts is a strategy for holding out against the banalities of romantic love; and even when that love overtakes them they persist in their satirical debunking, discarding a conventional lovers' discourse for mutual raillery.

There is also a more complex sense in which sexuality brings both body and language into play. Desire in Shakespeare is often a kind of obsession, a well-nigh monomaniacal fixation on another which tends to paralyse the self to a rigid posture. In this sense, it has something of the density and inertia of the body itself. But it also has the waywardness and promiscuity of language, sliding indifferently from one love-object to another, diffuse and self-divided in its workings. Desire plunges you into the body's depths and roots you to the spot, but it tends to shuttle you on soon enough to some other spot where you feel just as rooted. There is something anarchic about sexual desire which is to be feared, and the fear is less moral than political: in exposing the provisional nature of any particular commitment, Eros offers a potent threat to social order. And if desire is 'natural', then the unwelcome corollary of this is that it is natural for things to wander, deviate, stray out of place. This, as we have seen, is true of signs; and Shakespeare draws a close parallel between desire, language and money, both in their 'natural' errancy and in their homogenizing effect, the way they level out distinctive values and merge them into one amorphous mass of debased, near-identical objects:

> O spirit of love, how quick and fresh thou art!
> That, notwithstanding thy capacity
> Receiveth as the sea, nought enters there,
> Of what validity and pitch soe'er,
> But falls into abatement and low price
> Even in a minute. So full of shapes is fancy,
> That it alone is high fantastical.
>
> (*Twelfth Night*, I.i.9–15)

If sexuality is anarchic, then it would seem to require a repressive external authority to keep it firmly in place, as in *Measure for Measure*. But this will merely result in an eternal quarrel between libido and law. Instead, desire must find its own natural, stable form, known as the institution of marriage. Marriage is not an arbitrary force which coercively hems in desire, but reveals its very inward structure – what desire, if only it had known, had wanted all the time. When you discover your appropriate marriage partner you can look back, rewrite your autobiography and recognize that all your previously coveted objects were in fact treacherous, displaced parodies of the real thing, shadows of the true substance. This, broadly speaking, is the moment of the end of the comedies. Marriage is natural, in the sense of being the outward sign or social role which expresses your authentic inward being, as opposed to those deceitful idioms which belie it. It is the true language of the erotic self, the point at which the spontaneity of individual feeling and the stability of public institutions harmoniously interlock. It is at once free personal choice and impersonal bond, 'subjective' and 'objective' together, an exchange of bodies which becomes the medium of the fullest mutuality of minds. As such, marriage is the organic society in miniature, a solution to sexual and political dilemmas so ludicrously implausible that even Shakespeare himself seems to have had difficulty in believing it.

The action of *A Midsummer Night's Dream* is framed by the marriage of Theseus and Hippolyta, one instantly associated with money: Theseus complains in the play's opening lines that the slow-waning moon 'lingers my desires,/Like to a step-dame or a dowager,/Long withering out a young man's revenue.' What takes place within this frame, however, throws its official assumptions into radical question. If marriage is ideally the place where individual desire finds public sign and body, the play's actual sexuality is torn between a death-dealing, patriarchal public law on the one hand (Theseus and Egeus) and a purely random subjectivity of Eros on the other (the four interchangeable lovers). Demetrius, once united with Helena, speaks of having had his 'natural taste' restored to him, but the phrase borders on the oxymoronic: taste is 'natural' in the sense that there is no accounting for it, but its whimsicality makes it quite the opposite of Nature as a settled objective structure. Is love natural because it is so *fundamental* as to be inexplicable, or is it inexplicable because it is errantly subjective? What would seem 'natural' is the fact that all relationships are potentially reversible, as in the forest imbroglio; it may well be illusion (Oberon's magic) which brings this about, but the magic is an allegory of the misperceptions 'naturally' part of all human action. If Oberon's liquor literally induces characters to perceive each other differently, this after all is exactly what Theseus demands of the rebellious Hermia at the beginning of the play, to see through her father's eyes. The law is, in this sense, quite as fantastical as any fairyland hallucination, just as fairyland is quite as sadistically patriarchal as the court. If 'natural' relationships are disrupted by magical illusion and then benignly restored, this only goes to suggest that love – a matter of inexplicable preference – was bound up with illusion in the first place, a way of seeing which lacks objective grounds. Is loving Theseus really any less foolish than loving an ass? Indeed, without an admixture of deception (Oberon's magic in making Demetrius love Helena) the 'real' problems of the drama would not be resolved. Magical devices are thus structural to the play's 'realistic' conclusion, not mere supplementary aids to Nature. What matters in the end is not whether characters 'really' love each other or not – since anyone after all can love anyone else – but whether their illusions interlock. If they do, if the illusion is total, mutual and internally consistent, then this is perhaps the nearest we can approximate to truth or reality. Bottom's play fails to convince 'realistically' because the dramatic illusion is incomplete, disrupted as it is by bungling, well-intentioned asides to pacify the audience.

The bumptious Bottom is reluctant to confine himself to a single part in his drama, wishing to play several at once; and this, of course, is precisely what the lovers do in the forest, exchanging roles with dizzying speed. Each role, when lived, appears as absolute, only a moment later to be exposed as fortuitous. Social and sexual identities have the mystifying mutability of a paltering language or counterfeit currency: anything can be exchanged with anything else. This is particularly worrying for Shakespeare, since it seems like a grotesque caricature of his traditionalist belief that all identity is reciprocally constructed, constituted by social bonds and fidelities. This doctrine is a powerful weapon in his critique of bourgeois individualism, for which a man (as Coriolanus says of himself) is author of himself and knows no other kin. But if everyone is defined by what they are not, fashioned in relation to some other, does this not suggest an empty circularity of identities, ungrounded in any absolute? The circularity is acted out in a brief knockabout charade in the Trojan camp of *Troilus and Cressida*:

Achilles   . . . Come, what's Agamemnon?

Thersites   Thy commander, Achilles. Then tell me, Patroclus, what's Achilles?

Patroclus   Thy Lord, Thersites. Then tell me, I pray thee, what's Thersites?

Thersites   Thy knower, Patroclus. Then tell me, Patroclus, what art thou?

Patroclus   Thou must tell that knowest.

(II.iii.40–6)

To love is to live an imaginary identification with another, so that identity is always at once here and elsewhere, here *because* elsewhere; but if the self is always elsewhere it can err and be misappropriated, plunging you into self-estrangement. If identity is always partly 'other', then one can exert no full control over it; the self is radically 'split' from the outset, a prey to the capricious identifications of those with whom it identifies. When Bottom wears his ass's head there is a rift between how others view him and how he views himself, since he cannot see his own face; and the same is true of the revolving misperceptions of the four lovers, such that after Oberon's magic has gone to work, what Lysander is for Hermia (her lover, herself) is not what he is for himself (his beloved, Helena), nor what Helena is for herself (the rejected mistress of Demetrius), nor what Demetrius is for himself (Hermia's suitor).

The circuit of exchange, then, can be dislocated and reversed; but there would seem no 'outside' to it, no Other to this constant otherness, and so no fixed criteria of truth. The self is a commodity which lives only in the act of barter, love operating as the 'universal commodity' (Marx's term for money (or great equalizer of values. (It is also possible to be in love with love, just as one can be a miser; in|fact, Shakespeare suspects that there is an element of this in all erotic relationships.) If the self lives only in social exchange, then Shakespeare's defence of the feudal doctrine of mutuality against bourgeois individualism begins to look particularly ironic, since such individualism and commodity exchange go logically together. How is one to distinguish a 'good' reciprocity of selves, which for Shakespeare is bound up with a feudalist ideology of mutual bonds, from a 'bad' version of the same belief, in which all bonds are sundered by the frantic circulation of persons and things?

The society of *A Midsummer Night's Dream* is not, however, a mere groundless intersubjectivity. For intersubjectivity involves an otherness which remains personal (the alterity of one's lover), whereas desire in this drama is at root deeply impersonal. The play makes much of *looking*, of the insatiable lust of the eye, as symptomatic of the subjective nature of sexual attraction; but it would also seem to insinuate that what you look at, an ass or philanderer, does not really matter. In the play's fantasia of the unconscious, what looks through the individual eye is nothing less than the unconscious itself, casually indifferent to particular bodies, ransacking appearances in its desperate pursuit of some ultimate truth which refuses to be uncovered. The desire of the unconscious is bottomless, like the dream which it generates in Bottom; and this unfathomable place of the Other is figured within the text as the inhuman Puck, who can assume any shape or persona because he is nothing in himself. Puck is the delusive space towards which the hunters in the forest are drawn, even when they believe they are pursuing each other. Playing Lysander to Demetrius and Demetrius to Lysander, he becomes a vacant symbol within which desires congregate and collide, in one sense the controlling centre of the action, yet a centre which is absent, bodiless, eternally elusive. Puck mediates one character to the other, yet as the point where their false perceptions interlock he is necessarily quite unreal. Like desire itself, he is everywhere and nowhere, a trans-formative, teasingly ambiguous language in which assured identities are decomposed. And though such language, like the fairies themselves, is chimerical, it has the power to shape reality to its own ends. The fairies inhabit an autonomous world, but one which can intervene in human affairs as an alien force, and so with the impersonal quality of unconscious desire. Marx comments in *Capital* on the strange paradox whereby the mutual traffic of commodities exerts a determining force on real social relations; in this play, a domestic tiff between two metaphysical illusions has the power to derange the affairs of 'real' human beings.

Oberon and Puck, though mere figments themselves, disclose a desire concealed by 'fictive' social forms, and reveal it to be ridden with deception. The mechanicals, by contrast, hold to a naively empiricist sense of the relations between appearance and reality, breaking off their interlude to assure the wisecracking audience that this is not the real thing. Bottom may want to play several parts at once, but he is a grotesquely bad actor, unable to transcend the limits of his own stolid identity to perform anyone but himself. The ass's head is thus appropriate: like an animal, Bottom is unable to be either more or less than he is. He is thus the polar opposite of Puck, who has no existence outside his theatrical incarnations; Puck cannot be merely one thing, Bottom can be no more than one. This, once more, is a dualism of body and language, what Theodor Adorno called in a different context the 'torn halves of an integral freedom, to which however they do not add up'.[2] Bottom, for both good and ill, is too bodily to go beyond himself; Puck is pure transgression. The Athenian lovers themselves are a contradictory amalgam of the two, restless with sexual yearning unlike the phlegmatic Bottom yet, because constrained by the body, vulnerable to the havoc this wreaks as Puck is not. The 'solution', naturally enough, is marriage; but no sooner has the play concluded on this note than it thrusts its own chimerical nature before our attention in Puck's epilogue. If the hallucinated mismatchings of the forest are framed by the sober contract of marriage, that in turn is framed by self-conscious theatrical illusion. In foregrounding its own fictional character, the play wards off the disorderly desire it has itself unleashed; but it cannot do this without suggesting that its concluding nuptials are fictitious too. To dismiss itself nervously as a dream is no defence, since dreams are in one sense just as real as anything else. Reality secretes dreams as part of its very nature – just as it is 'natural' for that solid public institution the theatre to generate fantasies. It is difficult, then, for the play to defuse the seriousness of its content by branding it as illusion, since it has just spent five acts demonstrating that illusion is a very serious business indeed.

II

If desire tends to overwhelm any determinate signified or stable meaning with an excess of signifiers, then it is appropriate that Orsino at the opening of *Twelfth Night* should link it to music, an art form of the signifier alone, and one of which he wishes to surfeit and die. *Twelfth Night* is fascinated by the idea of words being torn from their material contexts to become self-generating, a tangled chain of metaphor which nowhere seems to button down on reality:

Sir Andrew	. . . Fair lady, do you think you have fools in hand?
Maria	Sir, I have not you by th'hand.
Sir Andrew	Marry, but you shall have; and here's my hand.

Maria	Now sir, thought is free. I pray you, bring your hand to the butt'ry bar and let it drink.
Sir Andrew	Wherefore, sweetheart? What's your meta-phor?
Maria	It's dry, sir.
Sir Andrew	Why, I think so; I am not such an ass but I can keep my hand dry. But what's your jest?
Maria	A dry jest, sir.
Sir Andrew	Are you full of them?
Maria	Ay, sir, I have them at my fingers' ends; marry, now I let go your hand, I am barren.

(I.iii.60–75)

Maria's speech is giddyingly free of fact ('thought is free'), hostile to the self-identity of things, an open space in which any bit of the world may combine kaleidoscopically with any other. 'A good wit', remarks Falstaff in *Henry IV, Part 2*, 'will make use of anything. I will turn diseases to commodity' (I. ii). Mystifying language like Maria's dispenses with a word's use value and converts reality into one sealed circuit of abstract exchange, just as the commodity form does with material goods. But this, as we have already seen, is something of a Pyrrhic victory for the imperial word, since in assimilating all things to itself it leaves the world empty, a 'nothing' which cannot be mastered, and before which it is struck impotent. A counter-move to this verbal colonialism is to assert baldly that things simply are what they are, as Sir Andrew Aguecheek does to forestall Sir Toby Belch's pedantic patter:

Sir Toby	Approach, Sir Andrew. Not to be abed after midnight is to be up betimes; and 'diluculo surgere' thou know'st –
Sir Andrew	Nay, by my troth, I know not; but I know to be up late is to be up late.
Sir Toby	A false conclusion! I hate it as an unfill'd can.

(II.iii.1–5)

Aguecheek's flat literalness forces you back, ironically, into
the dilemma you hoped to escape: a tautology is a worthless
self-identity which conveys nothing, leaving speech just as
self-referential as in Maria's quickfire metaphors.

The play's most professional pedlar of paradoxes, as
usual with Shakespeare, is the Clown, who actually calls
himself a 'corrupter of words':

> . . . To see this age! A sentence is but a chev'ril glove
> to a good wit. How quickly the wrong side may be
> turn'd outward! . . . I can yield you [no reason]
> without words, and words are grown so false I am
> loath to prove reason with them.

(III.i.10–12, 21–2)

Reason, the very form of reality, can be articulated only in
words, and yet is disfigured by them. Without language
there can be no reason, but no reason with it either; to
speak or keep silent, as Cordelia discovers, is equally
falsifying. What has discredited language in Feste's view is
commerce, the breaking of bonds: 'But indeed words are
very rascals since bonds disgrac'd them.' Bonds – written
commercial contracts – have rendered signs valueless, since
too often they are not backed by the physical actions they
promise; as the Duke complains in *Measure for Measure*:
'There is scarce truth enough alive to make societies secure,
but security enough to make fellowship accursed' (III.ii.)
To sport with language, the Clown suggests, is akin to
sexual promiscuity:

> *Viola*   . . .they that dally nicely with words may quickly
>   make them wanton.
> *Clown*   I would, therefore, my sister had no name, sir.
> *Viola*   Why, man?
> *Clown*   Why, sir, her name's a word; and to dally with
>   that word might make my sister wanton.

(III.i.13–18)

From thoughts of verbal fetishism and sexual desire, Feste
is led on logically to the topic of money. Having extracted
one coin from Viola, he then asks for another:

Clown	Would not a pair of these have bred, sir?
Viola	Yes, being kept together and put to use.
Clown	I would play Lord Pandarus of Phrygia, sir, to bring a Cressida to this Troilus.

(III.i.47–50)

Feste reifies the coins to living sexual partners, reducing himself to a mere pander between them; despite Viola's reminder about use value, money, the supposed servant of humanity, 'breeds' by its own promiscuous power. Bassanio in *The Merchant of Venice* piously denounces gold as 'thou pale and common drudge/'Tween man and man', but the truth would seem to be the opposite: human beings are no more than the humble mediators between commodities, transient occasions for their mutual exchange.

Where language becomes most dramatically manipulative in the play is in the duping of Malvolio, who is manoeuvred into his hamfisted courtship of Olivia by pure verbal illusion. Just as Olivia's supposed missive to him presents her as ruled by dead letters ('M.O.A.I. doth sway my life'), so this text itself rigorously governs Malvolio's sexual advances, right down to the ridiculous cross-garters and yellow stockings. Malvolio the servant, with his laboured petty-bourgeois preciseness of speech, overreaches his social role under the transgressive power of language, itself a 'servant' of humanity always apt to forget its place. Like Macbeth, Malvolio is seduced by a false linguistic coinage to exceed his 'proper' position. His bid for a higher freedom is ironically self-undoing, thrusting him into a materially cramping dungeon which, because pitch-dark, is also a kind of nothingness. By confining himself too exactly, pedantically obeying 'every point of the letter' which his enemies concoct, Malvolio hopes hubristically to transcend all restriction and become his mistress's lover. In the process he lands up in a prison where there is hardly space to move, yet whose darkness permits his imagination impotently free rein. As a steward, Malvolio's task is to expend and economize in good measure, neither jealously hoarding nor too lavishly dispensing. In fact, he lurches from an absurdly rigid adherence to his function to a wild extravagance of desire. We shall see a somewhat similar abrupt reversal in the Angelo of *Measure for Measure*.

Malvolio's social ambitiousness, like Macbeth's, threatens to eradicate the frontiers between illusion and reality, madness and sanity, word and thing. When individuals wander out of place, so does language; and for speech to unhinge itself from the world is another name for madness. This is evident enough when Feste and Sir Toby visit Malvolio in his prison, a scene reminiscent of Goldberg and McCann's tormenting of the hapless Stanley in Harold Pinter's *The Birthday Party*. The Clown disguises himself as a curate for the occasion, thus stacking four levels of illusion on top of each other: he is a Fool (itself a sort of nothing) assuming a role notorious for its hypocrisy ('I would I were the first that ever dissembled in such a gown') to visit a dungeon whose darkness renders his disguise superfluous. Having launched the fiction that Malvolio is mad, Feste solemnly treats this speculation as real, bringing 'rational' criteria to bear on it with a crazed exactitude not far from Malvolio's own. Because he controls the rules of the language game, any of Malvolio's responses can be turned against him as further proof of his lunacy:

> *Clown*   What is the opinion of Pythagoras concerning wild fowl?
>
> *Malvolio*   That the soul of our grandam might haply inhabit a bird.
>
> *Clown*   What think'st thou of his opinion?
>
> *Malvolio*   I think nobly of the soul, and no way approve his opinion.
>
> *Clown*   Fare thee well. Remain thou still in darkness: thou shalt hold th'opinion of Pythagoras ere I will allow of thy wits; . . .
>
> (IV.ii.48–53)

Malvolio cannot win: whatever actual utterance he produces

will be garbled and travestied by the rules of the game. Since 'objective' norms have been suspended, truth becomes a matter of who can destroy the other linguistically; the Clown scrupulously frames his questions to create double-binds for his victim ('But tell me true, are you not mad indeed, or do you but counterfeit?'), just as in Act V, scene i he tricks Fabian into cancelling out his own request to see a letter. When Malvolio tries to affirm his own sanity by comparing it with Feste's ('I am as well in my wits, fool, as thou art'), Feste can flick this to the boundary by exploiting the ambiguity of 'fool', as both social function and personal quality. 'Then you are mad indeed, if you be no better in your wits than a fool,' he retorts, negating his own sanity and Malvolio's along with it. Illusion can neutralize or put out of play any norm beyond its own closure, sucking into itself the whole of experience and so leaving nothing beyond its own boundaries which might be capable of negating it. No bit of 'real' evidence can falsify such verbal artefacts, since the artefact has always preprocessed the evidence and determined what counts as admissible. It is language, not just the dungeon, which appears as a prison-house.

That this is so is obvious enough in the 'duel' between Viola and Aguecheek. Just as Titania in *A Midsummer Night's Dream*, herself a fiction, is ensnared by Oberon into a further fantasy (her love for Bottom), so Aguecheek, having colluded in the plot against Malvolio, now finds himself on the receiving end of another of Sir Toby Belch's deceptions, in what could prove an infinite regress of victimage. By acting the role of slippery broker, mediating false information about each other to Viola and Sir Andrew, Belch's verbal chicanery fashions a dangerously real situation. As with coins and signs, the supposed go-between is the covert author of the event, breeding something from nothing, converting two negatives (each partner's reluctance to fight the other) into a spurious positive. In pressing Aguecheek to send a written challenge, Belch mischievously conflates texts and physical objects, suggesting that the larger the size of the paper the greater the insults will be:

Taunt him with the license of ink; if thou thou'st him some thrice, it shall not be amiss; and as many lies as will lie in thy sheet of paper, although the sheet were big enough for the bed of Ware in England, set 'em down; go about it. Let there be gall enough in thy ink, though thou write with a goose-pen, no matter. About it.

(III.ii.39–43)

He also persuades Aguecheek, a man renowned for the pathetic discrepancy between his words and deeds, that language ('a terrible oath') will frighten off his opponent as effectively as action.

As lord of linguistic misrule, Belch remains largely unscathed by his own mystifications. Like Falstaff he rejects social constraints, but does so in the name of a liberty to be, tautologically, no more than himself:

Maria   ... you must confine yourself within the modest limits of order.
Sir Toby Confine! I'll confine myself no finer than I am.

(I.iii.8–9)

Like Falstaff too he is a rampant hedonist, complacently anchored in his own body, falling at once 'beyond' the symbolic order of society in his verbal anarchy, and 'below' it in his carnivalesque refusal to submit his body to social control. He is thus at once more and less 'real' than those around him, full-bellied yet fantastical.

A similar paradox marks the Clown. The Fool interrogates all symbolic codes with his teasing double-talk, an eloquent void at the heart of social order. Yet this, precisely, is what he is hired for: since his role is to be roleless, his verbal licence is licensed. As Olivia comments, 'There is no slander in an allow'd fool.' As a corrupter of words, the Fool incarnates the pervasive falsity of social forms, and so is even less real than they are; but because he self-consciously performs what others live out unwittingly, he raises such negativity to the second power and becomes more real than those around him. As the Clown himself remarks, 'Those wits that think they have [wit] do very oft prove fools; and I that am sure I lack thee may pass for a wise man' (I.v.). To play the fool, Viola points out, requires a kind of wit; the Fool is an accomplished actor who, like Viola and unlike Orsino and Olivia, *consciously* assumes a dissembling mask and so remains admirably unmystified. Unlike Macbeth and Malvolio, he can blend subversive liberty with a secure social identity, and so can never overstep himself because what he is is pure transgression. This is only possible, however, because he appears to lack a body: the Clown, rather like Puck, is released from desire himself in imaging the unconscious of others.

Elsewhere in *Twelfth Night*, social roles come like language to determine the behaviour of their bearers. Olivia and Orsino, however 'genuine' their feelings may be, are both actors who perform their aloof or love-sick states as theatrical scripts from which their actions must never deviate. Each part feeds parasitically off the other, in an interlocking of illusions: Orsino's identity as rejected suitor depends upon Olivia's cultivated haughtiness, and vice versa. Viola, having assumed the fiction of disguise in the service of Orsino, is then drawn into this closed charade as pander or broker, acting the part of one actor (Orsino) to another actor (Olivia) in a way at odds with her own true identity (her love for Orsino). Like the Clown with his coins, she is reduced to a passive mediation between two fetishized fictions, an embodied verbal message or metaphor seeking to couple together two uncommunicating items. She confronts Olivia as an actress who must confine herself strictly to her text, disowning any personal identity beyond it:

> *Olivia* Whence came you, sir?
> *Viola*   I can say little more than I have studied, and that question's out of my part.
>
> (I.v.166–8)

When Viola asks to view Olivia's face, she is warned that

she is now 'out of [her] text'. It is writing which controls human behaviour, just as Olivia's countenance is presented in the form of a written inventory or set of mechanically itemized features.

Once entered into the closed cicuit of Orsino and Olivia, however, Viola does not remain a neutral presence. The messenger becomes the master, inspiring in Olivia a love which at once undercuts the artifice of her attitude to Orsino and in another sense is just as unreal: she does not know that Viola is a woman. The dialogue between the two women in Act III, scene i is plagued by this comic tension between their 'true' selves and their scripted performances, as both are forced into a 'bind' between them: if Viola plays her part successfully she wins Olivia for Orsino and so loses him for herself; in rejecting Viola as Orsino's apologist, Olivia must inevitably send packing the 'man' she loves. The 'true self' is intertwined with its pre-scripted models, just as surely as the real identities of things are confounded by the twists and tropes of language.

Throughout the play, the switchings and reversals of social roles act as a kind of dramatized metaphor: the physical doubling of Viola and her brother, for example, is a kind of visual pun. Hamlet's advice to the Players, to suit the action to the word and the word to the action, begins to look ludicrously utopian; instead, language devours and incorporates reality until it stands in danger of collapsing under its own excess. The signifier, whether of speech, money or desire, creates and dominates the signified; but as with the *Dream* the play can seize upon this troublesome fact to foreground its own fictive status, as when Fabian remarks that he would condemn Malvolio's behaviour as 'an improbable fiction' were he to see it on stage. When Viola (a boy playing a woman playing a man) confronts Olivia with Orsino's suit, an actor playing an actor playing an actor presents the case of one actor playing an actor to another doing just the same. It is doubtful that the institution of marriage will be enough to unravel these convolutions, whatever we are asked to believe in the final scene.

3   Law: *The Merchant of Venice, Measure for Measure, Troilus and Cressida*

I

It is a paradoxical fact about all language that it is at once entirely general and irreducibly particular. Any language can be viewed on the one hand as a system of relative regularities: we would not call a 'word' a mark which occurred only once. To be a word at all, it must have some given or potential location within the structure of language, some actual or possible place in the dictionary, which is independent of any single specific use of it. The same goes for the rules of language – syntax, semantics, and so on – which can be treated as purely formal conventions, independent of any concrete content. On the other hand, it is clear that all language is wholly particular, and that 'language in general' does not actually exist. Language is always this or that utterance in this or that situation. The paradox, then, is that actual speech or writing subverts the very generality of the structure which brings it into being.[1] What structural linguistics terms *parole*, the particular concrete utterance, in this sense trangresses the very *langue* (or general linguistic structure) which produces it. There is, in other words, something about language which always 'goes beyond': all discourse reveals a kind of self-surpassing dynamic, as though it were part of its very nature to be and do more than the dictionary can formulate. This is perhaps most evident in a poem, which deploys words usually to be found in the lexicon, but by combining and condensing them generates an irreducible specificity of force and meaning. A literary text is in one sense constrained by the formal principles of *langue*, but at any moment it can also put these principles into question. Language is a specific *event*, which cannot simply be read off from the formal structures which generate it.

If this is true of language, it is also true of law. For law to be law its decrees must be general and impartial, quite independent of and indifferent to any concrete situation. If this were not so we might end up with as many laws as there are situations, which would defeat the whole idea of law by violating its *comparative* nature, its attempt to apply the same general principles to widely different conditions. One law for one group and another law for another is commonly felt to be objectionable: it can lead to privilege, which literally means 'private law'. Yet the law, like language, 'lives' only in specific human contexts, all of which are unique. The gap between the general character of law and these unique individual contexts is bridged by the law's 'application'; but this, as with language, can never be a simple matter of reading off the rights and wrongs of a given action from the formal abstract tenets laid down in the statute book. Such application involves the creative *interpretation* of those tenets, and may well result in modifying or transforming them. As with language, the formal structure of the law generates certain events (verdicts, legal judgements, and the like) which may end up by undermining that structure. Legal case-history is not just a record of past 'applications' of the law, but a tradition of continuous reinterpretation of it which bears in forcibly on any current act of legal judgement.

In interpreting the law creatively, it is usually felt that one should have due regard to its 'spirit': judgements should be realistic and commonsensical, not narrowly technical or pedantic. Thus, in *The Merchant of Venice*, it is Shylock who has respect for the spirit of the law and Portia who does not. Shylock's bond does not actually state in writing that he is allowed to take some of Antonio's blood along with a pound of his flesh, but this is a reasonable inference from the text, as any real court would recognize. No piece of writing can exhaustively enumerate all conceivable aspects of the situation to which it refers: one might just as well claim that Shylock's bond is deficient because it does not actually mention the use of a knife, or specify whether Antonio should be sitting down, suspended from the ceiling or dressed in frilly knickerbockers at the time of cutting. Any text, that is to say, can be understood only by going beyond its letter, referring it to the material contexts in which it is operative and the generally accepted meanings which inform and surround it. Portia's reading of the bond, by contrast, is 'true to the text' but therefore lamentably false to its meaning. There is nothing 'false' about her reading in itself, which the text, taken in isolation, will certainly bear out; it is just that her interpretation is *too* true, too crassly literal, and so ironically a flagrant distortion. Portia's ingenious quibbling would be ruled out of order in a modern court, and Shylock (given that his bond were legal in the first place) would win his case.

The paradox, then, is that to preserve the structure of the law you must transgress what it actually says. By failing to do this, Portia threatens to bring the law into disrepute, skating perilously close to promoting 'private law' by a reading which is aberrant because too faithful. There is a ruthless precision about her sense of the text which exactly parallels Shylock's relentless insistence on having his bond. In this sense, one might claim, Shylock is triumphantly vindicated even though he loses the case: he has forced the Christians into outdoing his own 'inhuman' legalism. Indeed it is tempting to speculate that Shylock never really expected to win in the first place; he is hardly well placed to do so, as a solitary, despised outsider confronting a powerful, clubbish ruling class. One can imagine him waiting with a certain academic interest to see what dodge the

Christians will devise to let one of their own kind off the hook. Perhaps he throws the audience a knowing wink when Portia produces her knockdown argument. Shylock's curious reluctance to specify his motive in pursuing his suit, the oddly gratuitous quality of his vengeance, might be construed as evidence for this, as might one of his most crucially revealing declarations:

> The pound of flesh which I demand of him
> Is dearly bought, 'tis mine, and I will have it.
> If you deny me, fie upon your law!
> There is no force in the decrees of Venice.
>
> (IV.i.99–102)

It is almost as though Shylock is defying the court to deny him in order to expose its own hollowness. Either way he will win: by killing Antonio, or by unmasking Christian justice as a mockery. If the decrees of Venice were shown to be worthless, troubling political consequences might be in store for the state. To catch the Christians out in a *particular* juridical shuffle is of course to discredit the law in general, just as to lend out money gratis *à la* Antonio is to affect the general rate of exchange in the city. What is at stake in the courtroom, then, is less Shylock's personal desire to carve up Antonio than the law of Venice itself: will it maintain its proper indifference to individuals, penalize one of its own wealthy adherents at the behest of an odious Jew? The answer, of course, is that it will not; but in order to avoid doing so it must risk deconstructing itself, deploying exactly the kind of subjective paltering it exists to spurn. To protect itself, the law is forced into a hermeneutical errancy, the final consequence of which might be political anarchy. Shylock thus induces the Venetian law partly to undo itself, entering that alien system from the inside and operating its rules in a style which presses them towards self-contradiction. He takes 'for real' the dramatic charade of a system in which he has little faith, in order to uncover the genuine illusions at its heart.

That it should be the Christians who deny the spirit of

the law is, of course, deeply ironic, since they see themselves precisely as resisting Shylock's own hard-hearted legalism in the name of the 'human'. The 'human' is that which escapes the tyrannical precision of writing, the living voice of Portia's eloquence rather than the steely fixity of print. But this is absurd, since writing (legal bonds, commercial contracts, state decrees, marriage agreements) is of the very essence of Venetian society. In such a social order, who buys, eats, rules or cohabits is inescapably a question of script: there can be no appeal to some realm of purely 'human' values which lies quite beyond the letter. The human is not that which goes beyond writing, but the way in which writing, or language, goes beyond itself; writing itself is a matter of flesh and blood, as Antonio learns to his discomfort. One of the problems the play faces, then, is how to distinguish this positive mutual involvement of language and the body from that tyranny of the letter which destroys the body's substance. In one sense, written letters would seem more real than airy speech because they are material, and so rather like the physical body. The meaning or 'spirit' of such script then becomes analogous to the soul or consciousness, and like consciousness can enter into conflict with its material medium. In another sense it is 'breath' or living speech which is more aptly symbolic of the body, being a direct product of it. Speech, however, is passing and perishable, unfixed in contrast with script; and this unfixedness can cause it to deceive more readily than writing, which can always be used in evidence against you. Unlike Antonio's pledge, the lovers' vows to safeguard their mistresses' rings are not made in writing, and so may the more easily be broken; written contracts may oppress one in the lethal immutability of their letter, but by the same token they can protect you more efficiently against others' infidelity. In any case, as we have seen already, the immutability of print can be much exaggerated. The difficulty, then, would seem to be one of reconciling the warm yet perishable substance of breath with the necessary permanence and generality of a writing which constantly threatens to stifle it. Shylock warns Antonio that 'I'll have my bond, I will not hear thee *speak*'; Portia, by contrast, is all passionate eloquence. Any assumption that the latter is 'truer' than the former, however, is thrown into question by the fact that Portia is in disguise, considerably less disinterested than she appears, and intent on rescuing her lover's best friend by a quibble. Eloquence is never, it would seem, pure authentic presence; there is always an element of rhetorical artifice inseparable from it. The more intense their emotions, the more intricately florid the diction of Shakespeare's characters tends to grow.

Portia's courtroom speech in defence of Antonio is metaphorical excess in the service of crabbed literalness; and how to attain an acceptable measure between these two extremes is one of the play's preoccupations. The norm is defined by Nerissa, when she remarks to her mistress that 'they are as sick that surfeit with too much as they that starve with nothing' (I.ii.). Gratiano, who believes that 'silence is only commendable/In a neat's tongue dried, and a maid not vendible', speaks 'an infinite deal of nothing', in marked contrast to the glum taciturnity of Antonio, whose melancholy is (like unrequited love) the very image of an 'all' based on a negation. Melancholy, as Freud wrote, is mourning without an object: founded on some lack or loss, it pervades the whole of one's experience but, because apparently causeless, seems at the same time a pure void:

> In sooth, I know not why I am so sad.
> It wearies me; you say it wearies you;
> But how I caught it, found it, or came by it,
> What stuff 'tis made of, whereof it is born,
> I am to learn;
> And such a want-wit sadness makes of me
> That I have much ado to know myself.
>
> (I.i.1–7)

Melancholy is much ado about nothing, a blank, motiveless devaluation of the world. The less its cause can be identified the more acute the condition grows, feeding on its own indeterminacy; and the more acute the condition, the less definable its grounds. We have already seen such paradoxes of 'all' and 'nothing' associated in Shakespeare with money, and it is thus not accidental that Antonio is not only melancholic but a merchant – indeed *the* Merchant – of Venice. Melancholia is an appropriate neurosis for a profit-based society, discarding the use values of objects in order to plunder them for substance with which to nourish itself. Jaques in *As You Like It* can 'suck melancholy out of a song, as a weasel sucks eggs', reducing reality to empty husks to feed his gloomy narcissism.

Melancholy, then, overrides measure, but does so destructively. The play's more creative metaphor of such surplus value is mercy, which disregards the precise exchanges of credit and debt, crime and punishment, in a lavishly gratuitous (grace-like) gesture. This, of course, is what Portia requests of Shylock, who is sensible to be rather wary. For such gratuitousness is a deeply ambivalent quality: if it can creatively short-circuit the harsh equivalences of justice (an eye for an eye and a tooth for a tooth), it is also, one might claim, all very well for some. Those who wield power can afford to dispense with exact justice from time to time, since they, after all, control the rules of the game. It is less easy or intelligent for outcasts like Shylock, whose sole protection lies in the law, to conjure it away so cavalierly. The victimized need a fixed contract, however hard-hearted that may seem, precisely because they would be foolish to rely on the generosity of their oppressors, who are even more hard-hearted than print. If mercy is gratuitous, then the dispossessed can never quite know when their superiors are likely to be seized with a spontaneous bout of geniality. Gratuitousness, moreover, has a hint of Portia's perverse reading of the bond, an act which equally threatens to erode the essential impartiality of law.

The problem would seem to be that the formal, abstract character of the law is both necessary and reifying. It is necessary if social cohesion is to be sustained, since the law mediates diverse situations to each other by subsuming them under stable principles. Yet in doing so it threatens to erase what is specific about those situations, homogenizing vital differences as an inflexibly levelling force. The alternative to this would seem to be purely *ad hoc*, context-bound judgements of the Portia kind, bending general norms to fit particular instances. But this approach lands you in a kind of indifferentism ironically close to the one you were seeking to escape: by giving free rein to the signifier it would appear to license any interpretation you like, processsing and permutating the evidence to confirm a given theory. Anarchy and authoritarianism are not, after all, the binary opposites they seem: each returns a partial response to the problem of how to hold to consistent criteria while recognizing that they are likely to be transformed and transgressed. The hermeneutical dilemma posed by *The Merchant of Venice* could be seen as a conflict between licence and constraint. A true reading is at once constrained by the text and transgressive of it, neither flatly literal nor fancifully metaphorical. To interpret is to activate a set of codes; but part of what those codes will sometimes tell you is when to throw them aside and go beyond them, like ladders kicked away once mounted. Yet how does one discriminate between a productive 'going beyond' and a purely whimsical one? Where does one draw the dividing-line between a surplus which is fruitful and one which is mere inflation?

Some of the meaning of the play's curiously sharp focusing on the bond may be found in Shylock's magnificent protest against anti-semitism:

> I am a Jew. Hath not a Jew eyes? Hath not a Jew hands, organs, dimensions, senses, affections, passions, fed with the same food, hurt with the same weapons, subject to the same diseases, healed by the same means, warmed and cooled by the same winter and summer, as a Christian is? If you prick us, do we not bleed? If you tickle us, do we not laugh? If you poison us, do we not die? And if you wrong us, shall we not revenge? If we are like you in the rest, we will resemble you in that.
>
> (III.i.)

What individuals share most vitally in common is the body: it is by virtue of our bodies that we belong to each other, and no cultural or linguistic community which is not somehow founded upon this fact is likely to survive. For the texts in which Shylock trusts – the Old Testament – the body is not in the first place a physical object but a form of relationship, a principle of unity with others.[2] Shylock's ferocious insistence on having Antonio's flesh must be read in the light of his sufferings at the hands of anti-semites; not just as revenge for them – though this is no doubt one of his motives – but as a scandalous exposure of that which Antonio owes him – his body, an acknowledgement of common humanity with Shylock – and arrogantly denies. It is a matter of flesh and blood between the two men in every sense: the ritual carving up of Antonio, coolly appropriating part of his body, is a kind of black mass or grotesque parody of eucharistic fellowship. Shylock claims Antonio's flesh as his own, which indeed, in a sense which cuts below mere legal rights, it is; and the bond looms as large as it does because it becomes symbolic of this more fundamental affinity. To refuse Shylock his bond means denying him his flesh and blood, and so denying *his* flesh and blood, his right to human recognition. The bond, in one sense destructive of human relations, is also, perversely, a sign of them; the whole death-dealing conflict between the two men is a dark, bitter inversion of the true comradeship Shylock desires, the only form of it now available to him. The impersonal absolutism of his pursuit of the bond parodies the absoluteness and impersonality of the bonds which link us to a common humanity, and which no mere subjective whim can set aside. Shylock makes out his deal with Antonio to be a friendly one ('this is kind I offer'), an assessment not entirely tongue-in-cheek: the usurer, astonishingly, is setting aside his customary credit and debt calculations for an object which is literally worthless, not even as profitable as mutton. There is a bizarre gratuitous-ness about Shylock's bargain, which demands both more and less than he would normally ask in such matters;

indeed Antonio himself thinks the deal a generous one, though Bassiano doesn't share his opinion. Shylock breaks with his usual business code to give Antonio special treatment: he demonstrates favouritism and partiality, risking a bad exchange. It may seem perverse to 'favour' someone by having him pledge his life to you, but the alternative to this 'all' is nothing, since Antonio may well go scot-free. The bond is a 'merry sport', a pointless jape or exuberant fiction so monstrous in its implications that it is hard to take it seriously, so excessive of all customary measure as to mean nothing.

Like jesting, the bonds of human solidarity are beyond all reason. There is no reason of a calculative kind why human beings should respond to each other's needs: it is just part of their 'nature', constitutive of their shared physical humanity, that they should do so. Shylock implicitly makes this point before the Venetian court when he stubbornly refuses to provide a rationale for his apparently inhuman behaviour:

> As there is no firm reason to be rend'red
> Why he cannot abide a gaping pig;
> Why he, a harmless necessary cat;
> Why he, a woollen bagpipe, but of force
> Must yield to such inevitable shame
> As to offend, himself being offended;
> So can I give no reason, nor I will not,
> More than a lodg'd hate and a certain loathing
> I bear Antonio, that I follow thus
> A losing suit against him. Are you answered?
>
> (IV.i.53–62)

The closest analogy to the 'inexplicable' demands of our common physical humanity is, ironically, the pure subjectivism of 'taste' or prejudice. 'Human nature', in the sense of the mutual needs and responsibilities which spring from our sharing in the same material life, is for Shakespeare the measure of all significant language and action, but itself escapes such measure; it is the 'ground' of our social life which cannot itself be grounded. It is thus both 'objectively' determining and, paradoxically, as resistant to rational enquiry as a merry sport or a fear of cats. Shylock values Antonio's worthless flesh immeasurably more than the sum Antonio has pledged, and refuses to be bribed by Portia; and he is, of course, right to believe that human flesh and blood cannot be quantified. That which is nugatory, beyond all measure, is also that which is most precious, as the ambiguous term 'invaluable' would suggest. It is Antonio himself who is the quantifying bourgeois, and Shylock who stands up for a more traditional conception of bonds and values.[3] Shylock's action cuts against bourgeois Venice in two opposed ways. On the one hand, it manifests a 'gratuitousness', with its special regard for an individual and its partiality in hatred, which defies the abstract quantifications of both law and money. On the other hand, it is performed in the name of an impersonal human bonding which makes no whimsical dispensations for individuals. Shylock thus behaves in an apparently capricious way to reveal the absolutely binding nature of a common humanity: Portia acts with parallel whimsicality to ward off such a recognition.

For the worthless to become most precious is also the point of the casket scenes at Belmont, where the relative values of lead and gold are inverted. If Shylock refuses gold, so does Bassanio; both prefer flesh and blood – in Bassanio's case, Portia's. But for Bassanio to obtain Portia is also of course for him to grow rich. Having improvidently thrown his money around, Bassanio has come to Belmont to buy up the well-heeled Portia with the aid of Antonio's loan, rashly jeopardizing his friend's life in the process; but there is nothing surprising in the way this self-loving parasite then elevates love over riches in the very act of purchasing a woman. Such romanticism, with its sancti-monious talk of the inestimability of love, is just the other side of the commercial coin: the bourgeoisie have always pretended that sex transcends utility, at the very moment they debase it to a commodity. The Romantic is in this respect just the flipside of the Utilitarian, fetishizing a realm (the love of a good woman) supposedly free of his own squalid transactions. 'The bourgeois viewpoint,' Marx comments, 'has never advanced beyond this antithesis between itself and this romantic viewpoint, and therefore the latter will accompany it as its legitimate antithesis up to its blessed end.'[4] The irony of this is that the very qualities in which love is thought to transcend money – its measurelessness, transmutability, inexplicable mystery – are the very characteristics of money itself. Money is less the opposite of erotic desire than its very image. Indeed Bassanio makes this point himself when he compares love to an inflated language, a phenomenon which, as we have seen, is for Shakespeare akin to commercial dealings:

> Madam, you have bereft me of all words;
> Only my blood speaks to you in my veins;
> And there is such confusion in my powers
> As, after some oration fairly spoke
> By a beloved prince, there doth appear
> Among the buzzing pleased multitude,
> Where every something, being blent together,
> Turns to a wild of nothing, save of joy
> Express'd and not express'd. . . .
>
> (III.ii.176–84)

A man in debt, like Bassanio, is actually 'worse than nothing'; has, as it were, a negative value. But the magic of capital investment can transfigure such nothing into everything.

The casket scenes, then, represent the acceptably idealist face of mercantile society, with their naive contrasts of appearance and reality. Shakespeare rejects any simple counterpointing of the two, believing in what Lenin once called the 'reality of appearances'. In this society, flesh and blood are inescapably bound up with profit and loss, in the selling of a daughter as much as in the maiming of Antonio. At Belmont, money is a question of measure, whereas love is 'free'. Shylock does not share this false consciousness: for him, love is not the subjectivist whims of Eros but the ruthlessly impersonal requirements of *agape* (charity), which demands precise services, obligations and recognitions. These properly impersonal constraints allow no room for 'freedom': the racist Antonio is not in fact free to kick Shylock around like a dog, since all individuals have an equal claim on one's humanity regardless of their race or other distinguishing features. There is something necessarily abstract about charity, just as there is about the law. Portia thinks that mercy is free, 'not strained' (constrained), but this is surely dubious: mercy must not, for example, be allowed to make a mockery of justice. It belongs to justice to make recompense for injuring another, which mercy may temper but cannot cavalierly wish away. Would it have been admirably merciful, or an obscene insult to the dead, to have allowed a later anti-semite, Adolf Eichmann, to go free? Should one cease to press for justice even though one's actions unavoidably injure one's oppressors?

The impartiality of law, then, must act as a symbolic embodiment of the impersonal claims of human justice and charity. The law of Venice, of course, does nothing of the kind, even before Shylock intervenes to deconstruct it: it is class law, as Shylock himself makes brutally clear:

> You have among you many a purchas'd slave,
> Which, like your asses and your dogs and mules,
> You use in abject and in slavish parts,
> Because you bought them; shall I say to you
> 'Let them be free, marry them to your heirs –
> Why sweat they under burdens? – let their beds
> Be made as soft as yours, and let their palates
> Be season'd with such viands'?

(IV.i.90–7)

If the Duke is worried about refusing Shylock his pound of flesh, it is because, as Antonio comments, the thing will look bad in the eyes of foreign businessmen. The problem, however, is that the law would seem able to sustain its proper impartiality, and so buttress social order, only at the cost of a frigid indifference to particular cases which estranges it from common humanity and so paradoxically risks a *collapse* of social order. There would appear in this sense to be something self-deconstructive about the law, which tends to frustrate its own ends in the very act of trying to promote them. The law necessarily abstracts and equalizes, and so tyrannizes over 'flesh and blood' in the sense of concrete human situations, even as, at another level, it embodies the 'bonds' of that humanity. But if this uniformity is thrown aside for purely *ad hoc* or *ad hominem* judgments, then each situation becomes autonomous (literally, a 'law unto itself') and so just as absolute in its own way as the law it sought to replace. What is lost by this move is the comparative evaluation of different conditions, which then become as tautological as the self-referring sign. Indeed logically speaking we would then not even be able to speak of a 'condition', for one condition is identifiable only if it can be roughly demarcated from another. True law is, so to speak, metaphorical, seeking a balance of similarities and differences; but this fine tension, as with all metaphor, can always split apart in either direction, reducing unique situations to singular identity or fostering – what is strictly unthinkable – a cult of pure difference. Angelo in *Measure for Measure* goes for the former option; Lucio for the latter.

II

That anarchy and authoritarianism are not quite the contraries they seem is made dramatically obvious in *Measure for Measure* by Angelo's sudden about-turn from repressive legalist to rampant lecher. But this *volte face* is not as mysteriously inexplicable as it may seem. For one thing, a purely abstract or formal law, unresponsive to the claims and impulses of the body, becomes detached from desire, including its own, and such desire may consequently run unchecked. In this sense Angelo enacts in his own person the rift between law and desire in Vienna as a whole: frigidly unyielding to flesh and blood, the law he incarnates is unconstrained by sensuous needs and so a blank space open to being inscribed by the body, captivated by Isabella's sexual attractiveness, in the most negative way. For another thing, law and desire share a similar quality of indifference: Angelo's lust for Isabella's body is as ruthlessly impersonal as the levelling categories of law, for which bodies are also in a certain sense interchangeable. More-over, the play makes it clear that law actually *breeds* desire as well as blocks it.[5] The law is not simply repressive, a negative prohibition placed upon the will; what is desired is precisely what is most strictly tabooed, and the taboo perversely intensifies the yearning. It is Isabella's chaste untouchability which fuels Angelo's passion, so that desire and prohibition become mutually ensnared, apparent opposites which are in truth secret conditions of one another:

> . . . it is I
> That, lying by the violet in the sun,
> Do as the carrion does, not as the flow'r,
> Corrupt with virtuous season. Can it be
> That modesty may more betray our sense
> Than woman's lightness? Having waste ground
>   enough,
> Shall we desire to raze the sanctuary,
> And pitch our evils there? O, fie, fie, fie!
> What dost thou, or what art thou, Angelo?
> Dost thou desire her foully for those things
> That make her good?
>
> (II.ii.165–75)

Excessive restraint breeds libertinism, just as a glut of liberty leads to restraint:

> *Lucio*   Why, how now, Claudio, whence comes this
>   restraint?
> *Claudio* From too much liberty, my Lucio, liberty;
>   As surfeit is the father of much fast,

> So every scope by the immoderate use
> Turns to restraint. Our natures do pursue,
> Like rats that ravin down their proper bane,
> A thirsty evil; and when we drink we die.
>
> (I.ii.118–24)

There is another important sense in the play in which law and flesh and blood are not simply to be counterpointed. In refusing to sacrifice her chastity for her brother's life, Isabella would seem to elevate an abstract moral absolute over the immediate claims of humanity. Critics have accordingly complained about the prudishness with which she is prepared to exchange Claudio's head for an intact hymen. But this is to misunderstand the subtle relations between the essential generality of law and its particular instances. If you compromise a principle in one pressing situation for the sake of flesh and blood, then you ineluctably compromise the security of all the flesh and blood which takes shelter beneath that principle. If Angelo is allowed to get away with his sexual schemings in this instance, what woman in Vienna is safe? Then indeed the ruling class may be permitted to treat all women's bodies as their private possessions. Just as a particular commercial bargain may alter the general rates of exchange which govern it, so more than one woman's virginity is at stake in turning down Angelo's deal.

As its title suggests, *Measure for Measure* is much concerned with the question of exchange values, epitomized in the strict interchanges of an impersonal justice which disregards particular qualities. The law must lay aside specific bonds of friendship or favouritism:

> It is the law, not I, condemn your brother.
> Were he my kinsman, brother, or my son,
> It should be thus with him.
>
> (II.ii.80–2)

Isabella's response to the 'precise' Angelo's stern impartiality is to point out that all human beings are sinful:

If he had been as you, and you as he,
You would have slipp'd like him; but he, like you,
Would not have been so stern.

(II.ii.76–8)

This is hardly a knockdown argument: all Isabella claims, in a useless tautology, is that if Angelo had been Claudio he would have behaved like him. To reason in this way is to retreat to the autonomous individualism and self-referentiality of 'private law' – which is no law at all, and which, as we have seen, is just as absolute and self-grounding in its own way as autocratic legalism. The law then becomes a kind of private language, which is a contradiction in terms. Even Elbow's crashing malapropisms ('respected' for 'suspected', and so on) gather a clear enough public meaning from their contextual consistency, tracing within themselves the shadow of the 'normative' social term from which they deviate. The case Isabella is fumbling for is not the vacuously self-evident point that if Angelo was Claudio he would be Claudio, but that all individuals, because of their shared moral frailty, are in some fundamental sense equal and interchangeable: because we all sin we should be ready to forgive sin in others. Angelo rejects this plea out of hand:

You may not so extenuate his offence
For I have had such faults; but rather tell me,
When I, that censure him, do so offend,
Let mine own judgement pattern out my death,
And nothing come in partial.

(II.i.27–31)

What Angelo fails to see here is that this closed circuit of mutual recriminations could be made to cancel itself out: why not flip this vicious circle over at a stroke and transform it into a virtuous circle of mutual forgiveness? Why should not a negative reciprocity of values be inverted into an affirmative one, two negatives make a positive, our common weakness become the ground of mercy rather than censure? If everyone condemns everyone else because they may be arraigned themselves, then this pointlessly self-supporting structure could be turned inside out, and everyone exculpate each other in just as groundlessly ritual a way. For Angelo, however, this would make a mockery of justice. The fact that I am morally weak is no logical bar to my judging such weakness in others, just as the fact that I am a hopeless football player does not prevent my appreciating fine or foul play as a spectator. It is an individualist mistake, a Romantic fetishizing of 'private' experience, to believe that we can only judge accurately of that of which we have direct inward knowledge. Besides, the fact that I am in principle capable of the crimes of those I accuse does not mean to say that I have actually committed them, and so disenfranchised myself from judgement; mercy would seem rather too abstract in this respect, too inattentive to the faults which the judge actually has. Angelo, who is by no means a straw target as a moral theorist, believes that if we simply forgave each other all the time we would be allowing the 'inherent' meaning and value of particular actions to be smothered in a sentimental subjectivism which attended less to what was materially 'there' than to the quality of our response to it. And this would just be a more subtle form of abstraction than the relentlessly impersonal operations of justice.

The ironic flaw in Angelo's position, however, is that if we were really to attend to 'inherent' values and meanings, to see things as they really are without the subjectivist squint of mercy, we would actually be compelled to forgive each other all the time. This, indeed, is the best card Isabella plays:

> Alas! alas!
> Why, all the souls that were were forfeit once;
> And He that might the vantage best have took
> Found out the remedy. How would you be
> If He, which is the top of judgement, should
> But judge you as you are?
>
> (II.ii.73–8)

If you do in fact estimate individuals as they truly are, then nobody would ever get off at all; 'use every man after his desert,' Hamlet comments, 'and who shall scape whipping?' Christ, it would seem, is clement only by a calculated moral squint, systematically refusing to judge us as we are. To treat someone 'as they are' may be at the deepest level to treat them as representative, just as the law does, but in this case representative of the moral fragility of humankind in general, and so conveniently combining the law's abstract generality with a sympathetic understanding of particular flesh and blood. In this way one might hope to avoid both legalistic and partial judgements at a stroke. The harsh indifference of the law might be made to work against itself without lapsing into mere merciful whimsy, for mercy, properly understood, is just as remorselessly impersonal a claim on our humanity as is justice. Indeed, in one sense it is more abstract than justice as it actually *overlooks* particularities, pretends that they are not there.

The problem, however, is how this global undercutting of exact exchanges is to be distinguished from indifference in its most negative, Lucio-like sense. Lucio is an ethical naturalist whose complacent appeal to the body cynically subverts all values. 'Flesh and blood' can mean the body as biological given, whose appetites may be endorsed simply because they are there. Or it can be a normative rather than a descriptive term, meaning a solidarity with human infirmities which none the less, through the discriminations of justice, acknowledges them as such rather than, like Lucio, nonchalantly turning a blind eye. Forgiveness is valuable precisely because it is difficult: it means bearing with others *despite* a recognition of the injuries they have done you. Lucio's man-about-town cockiness is thus a caricature of the virtue, valueless because it does not have to pay for its tolerance. There can be a worthless sort of mercy: as the Duke comments, 'When vice makes mercy, mercy's so extended/That for the fault's love is th'offender friended' (IV.ii.107–8). In a similar way, Isabella distinguishes 'lawful mercy' from the 'ignominy in ransom' or 'foul redemption', which is Angelo's distortion of it. Mercy is not mere gratuitousness: to be *too* free, as with Lucio's abusive tongue, is to wound and constrain others. Justice and mercy must be blended together rather like precision and creativity in language: to be too precise like Angelo is to reify law and language to a fixed transcendental sense, ignoring the creative 'surplus' or surpassing of the norm which all actual speech and judgement involves. But that surplus must not be allowed to exceed the measure to the point where it undercuts it entirely, for then there would be no finely discriminated situations to be forgiving *about*.

Lucio's cynical indifference is paralleled in the play by the astonishing moral inertia of Barnadine, a Musil-like psychopath so careless of life that he objects to being executed only because it interrupts his sleep. Death, in a familiar cliché, is the great leveller, reducing all exact values and distinctions to nothing, and Barnadine gains a curiously enviable freedom by appropriating this future state into the present, as an image of living death. If he is unperturbed by the thought of execution, it is in a sense because he is dead already, living at that end-point where all odds are struck even. The state must defer his dying until he has been persuaded to accept it willingly, otherwise the punishment will have no point. Unless Barnadine somehow 'performs' his own death, it will not constitute an event in his life and so will discredit the law that has inflicted it upon him. There is no more effective resistance to power than genuinely not caring about it, since power only lives in exacting a response of obedience from its victims. The play distinguishes this biological indifference from what it sees as an authentic living towards death, of the kind Claudio finally comes to embrace: 'If I must die,/I will encounter darkness as a bride/And hug it in my arms' (III.i.). The suicide and the martyr look alike, but are in fact opposites: the one throws away his life because he judges it worthless, the other surrenders his most valuable possession. The martyr becomes something by actively embracing nothing; the suicide simply substitutes one negativity for another. Though death finally erases all measure and distinction, you must cling provisionally to those values while you live, just as mercy ultimately undercuts the tit for tat of justice but must not be permitted to undo those mutualities completely.

The chief form of tit for tat in the play is a ceaseless exchange and circulation of bodies: Angelo's for the Duke's, Isabella's (so Angelo hopes) for Claudio's, Barnadine's for Claudio's, Mariana's for Isabella's. Bodies are a kind of language, which can either falsify (as in the bed trick with Mariana) or involve a just and proper correspondence. The final distribution of bodies to their appropriate positions is the event of marriage, with which the play concludes. Yet no unblemished justice can ever quite be achieved, since no two things are exactly identical and so can never effect a purely equitable exchange. If x is equivalent to y, then we have proclaimed in the same breath that x is not in fact y, superimposed similitude on difference. No one term can fully represent another, just as Angelo cannot entirely incarnate the absent Duke, since a total identity of both terms would spell the death of representation itself. There is always, in other words, some residue of difference, dislocation or disparity in any proper exchange which threatens to undo it; and something of the play's notoriously factitious conclusion may well spring from this fact.

But there are also other senses in which *Measure for Measure* can never quite attain the ideal towards which it strives: a judicious balance of justice and mercy, precision and superfluity, equivalence and unique identity, general and particular, inherent and imputed values. The law must be above sin; yet since no human being is without sin it would seem inherently estranged from flesh and blood. The law tends naturally towards reification, caught in a cleft stick between its abstract edicts and its particular objects. To uphold its generality you must treat particular cases as exemplary; but this means punishing Claudio for a vice which 'all ages smack of'. Isabella, who represents a general principle to Angelo in her own person, finds that she has seduced him by her person rather than by the principle. One individual may justifiably penalize another if he is himself guiltless of that particular offence; but taken as a whole the human race cannot pass judgement on itself, since this would be as pointlessly tautological as someone placing himself under arrest. The rigorously impersonal transactions of justice must be maintained, if social order is not to crumble; but the mercy which is officially 'supplementary' to that justice threatens to erode it from the inside, and it is within this irresolvable tension that humanity must live. They must cling to the centrality of measure and normativity, while recognizing in a difficult double optic that these things are ultimately groundless. Forgiveness – the active forgoing of exact equivalences, the gratuitous rupture of the circuit – is the trace of this final groundlessness (which is also the future levelling of death) within the regulated symmetries of the present. The most effective spur to being sinless oneself, it might be cynically considered, is that it grants you a title to pass judgement on others; virtue in oneself would thus seem linked to vice in others, just as mercy would seem to flourish on sin (since one's own immorality is the offender's hope for forgiveness). A thoroughly vicious ruler who acknowledged his own moral turpitude would appear to be the criminal class's best guarantee for a troublefree life. The choice would seem to be between this politically undesirable solution, a relatively sinless ruler who none the less exercised clemency, and a prince who did not regard his own moral laxity as any obstacle to executing the law. The latter solution divorces the general and particular too sharply, resulting in a reified authority which is bad for social harmony; the second possibility is the ideal one, but frustratingly difficult to achieve precisely because mercifulness springs from an inward sympathy with sin, and a virtuous exponent of it thus begins to sound like a contradiction in terms. Shakespeare's quandary is a version of Bertolt Brecht's, who once remarked wryly that only somebody inside a situation could judge it, and he was the last person who could judge. It is all very well to speak of a prudent balance of justice and mercy; but how is the necessarily transcendental principle of the law to avoid being corroded and contaminated by the specific perplexities it has to sort out? How is mercy to break the vicious circle of prosecutions when it must somehow spring from inside that circle, from a humble solidarity with vice? If that censorious circularity is indeed transformable into a community of mutual acceptance, from what vantage-point – inside or beyond the circuit, or at its very edge – can this be effected? These are not, finally, questions which the play can satisfactorily answer. Instead, we are told that people get married, even though marriage, which as we have seen already is an undecidable merging of gratuitous affection and inherent propriety, is part of the very problem to which it is being proposed as a solution.

III

Perhaps one of the central puzzles confronting *Measure for Measure* can be summarized in this way. In order to preserve political stability, you need that fine mutuality of values which is justice; yet to achieve this mutuality requires an abstract, overarching structure (law), and the very abstractness of this structure tends to strip situations of their determinate qualities, rendering them arbitrarily interchangeable with each other, and thus fostering a mutability which helps to undermine political order. In this sense law operates rather like money, language and desire: all of these systems involve exchange and equivalence, which is in itself a stabilizing factor; but because they are necessarily indifferent as systems to particular objects or uses, they tend to breed an anarchic state of affairs in which everything blurs indiscriminately into everything else, and the system appears to be engaging in transactions for its own sake. There is, in other words, something in the very structures of stability themselves which offers to subvert them, something in the very fact of being 'precise' which leads, as in Angelo's case, to manic disorder.

In seeking to oppose Angelo's absolutism, Isabella, despite her belief that 'truth is truth to the end of reckoning', draws at one point on a linguistic analogy: 'That in the captain's but a choleric word/Which in the soldier is flat blasphemy' (II.ii.130–1). Context, in short, defines meaning: the meaning of a word is not some fixed, inherent property, but simply its various uses in particular situations. Shakespeare himself by no means entirely endorses Isabella's case, however, for good reasons of his own. For his work makes it clear that such a 'contextualism' of meaning, pressed to a logical extreme, would result in just the kind of relativism he sees as inimical to political cohesion. Take Isabella's point a few steps further and we might all end up as Elbows, privately legislating Humpty Dumpty-wise the meaning of our own words. For Shakespeare, it is the consistency or self-identity of a term from context to context which determines its proper meaning, just as it is consistency which is usually in his plays the most suggestive index of human sanity. (It is the 'dependency of thing on thing' in Isabella's discourse which, the Duke says, persuades him that she is not mad.) This is not to say that Shakespeare ignores the plurality of contexts in which a word can be used; it is just that he believes that any actual use of it must be consistent with a more general context even if it goes beyond it, just as any specific application of the law must balance a respect for general principles with sensitivity to a particular state of affairs. There seems little doubt that in *Troilus and Cressida* Shakespeare sides with Hector against Troilus in their heated exchange over the question of Helen's value:

> *Hector*   Brother, she is not worth what she doth cost
> The keeping.
> *Troilus*   What's aught but as 'tis valued?
> *Hector*   But value dwells not in particular will:
> It holds his estimate and dignity
> As well wherein 'tis precious of itself
> As in the prizer. . .
>
> (II.ii.51–7)

Hector wants a fusion of intrinsic and assigned values, so that he can use the 'given' qualities of things as a norm for assessing other people's value-judgements. This, at least, is what Ulysses does later in the play:

> Nature, what things there are
> Most abject in regard and dear in use!
> What things again most dear in the esteem
> And poor in worth!
>
> (III.iii.127–30)

Troilus, by contrast, holds to an existentialist rather than essentialist theory of value, as is clear from his hot retort when Helen's worth is questioned:

> Is she worth keeping? Why, she is a pearl
> Whose price hath launch'd above a thousand ships,
> And turn'd crown'd kings to merchants.
>
> (I.ii.)

Troilus means formally that Helen has launched a thousand ships because she is a pearl, but there is an implication that she is a pearl *because* she has done so; it is the activity she has given rise to which confers value upon her, not her inherent value which justifies that activity. Pearls, after all, are valuable because their rarity involves a good deal of labour in obtaining them, not because they have (like, say, water) some intrinsic property beneficial to humanity. But if Helen is precious because she is the focus of such admirable strivings, must not Troilus be implicitly invoking certain 'objective' standards of value to decide that such strivings are admirable in the first place? The question of value, in short, is merely pushed one stage back, and nothing is actually resolved.

If this is a difficulty with appeals to merely 'conjunctural' value – that they would always seem implicitly to evoke more general norms even in the act of denying them – there would seem another kind of problem with the absolute standards of Hector and Ulysses. For these standards, by which particular situations can be judged, always turn out to be no more than the distilled experience of previous situations. To claim that the use of a word in a specific context must be governed by its 'inherent' meaning is just to say that this particular context must be related to others. Any general principle can thus be deconstructed into an accumulated set of discrete particulars. A 'given' or 'inherent' value simply means what others – perhaps in the past – have held to be precious, and thus risks losing its transcendental authority. To state what something 'really' means is just to report on the ways other people have happened to use the word; all meaning is in this sense dialogic or 'intertextual'. If this is so, then the well-ordered norms which Shakespeare would seem to desire merely push the problem of relativism back a stage. All that can be appealed to against the subjectivism of a Troilus is simply a wider intersubjectivity, which cannot be anchored in anything beyond itself.

The paradigm of a fixed value would seem to be a thing's absolute identity with itself, as in this bantering exchange between Pandarus and Cressida:

Pandarus   Well, I say Troilus is Troilus.
Cressida   Then you say as I say, for I am sure he is not Hector.
Pandarus   No, nor Hector is not Troilus in some degree.
Cressida   'Tis just to each of them: he is himself.
(I.ii.65–8)

This is hardly Shakespeare's most richly exploratory piece of dialogue. To describe what something 'really' is inevitably involves you in contextualizing comparisons; simply to call something an apple is already to have assigned it to a general class of objects, which are what they are because they are not, say, bananas. Troilus, who disdains comparisons and holds romantically to the unique quality of things, replies to Aeneas's enquiry, 'Wherefore not afield?' with the profoundly informative, 'Because not there' (I.i.). Achilles' stiff-necked pride is a refusal to define himself in any terms beyond his own being, the futile circularity of self-conferred, publicly unwarranted value: 'He that is proud eats up himself' as Agamemnon remarks (II.iii.). Achilles' privatized, grossly inflated scale of values ('Things small as nothing, for request's sake only,/He makes important' (II.iii.)) may be contrasted with Diomed's shrewdly measured estimation of Helen, a most untypical burst of judiciousness for this play:

> For every false drop in her bawdy veins
> A Grecian's life has sunk; for every scruple
> Of her contaminated carrion weight
> A Troyan hath been slain.

> (IV.i.71–4)

Once you begin weighing and comparing, however, the object whose value you sought to determine is no longer identical with itself: it is 'differed' by your speech, inscribed within a context of otherness, and the danger is that there is in principle no end to such differencing. What then becomes of the integrity of the very thing you seek to judge? If Agamemnon is Achilles' commander, Achilles Thersites' lord, Thersites Patroclus's knower and so on, then where does the metaphorical chain of mutually definitive items stop? Ulysses warns the languidly *dégagé* Achilles that 'no man is the lord of anything,/Though in and of himself there be much consisting,/Till he communicate his parts to others' (III.iii.116–17). Social relations are not simply the medium within which an individual may choose to express his already well-formed identity, but the very discourse which constitutes that self. Others are, so to speak, the signifiers which produce the signified of oneself. But if this social emphasis guards against the tautology of possessive individualism, it does so only at the cost of dividing and destabilizing identity, dwindling it to a mere effect of the Other. It would appear that the self, like signs and values, has no choice between being fully, autonomously itself, which is a kind of nothing, and being a shifting cypher wholy dependent on context, which is another kind of nothing.

This is also a dilemma in respect of the self's history. If history furnishes you with a norm or standard beyond the existential moment, it also tends to dissolve on closer inspection into no more than a cumulative series of such fleeting instants. This is the point of Ulysses' great speech on time, which reduces history to so much dead weight to be shucked off at each new moment:

> Time hath, my lord, a wallet at his back,
> Wherein he puts alms for oblivion,
> A great-siz'd monster of ingratitudes.
> Those scraps are good deeds past, which are devour'd
> As fast as they are made, forgot as soon
> As done. Perseverance, dear my lord,
> Keeps honour bright. To have done is to hang
> Quite out of fashion, like a rusty nail
> In monumental mock'ry.

(III.iii.)

The logical strain of this is apparent: Ulysses urges perseverance – pursuing a consistent project over time – in the very act of deconstructing such continuities into an eternal present. If the past is oblivion, what are you persevering *in*, and who is doing the persevering? The ideal way to live, in a familiar Romantic paradox, would be constantly to teeter on the brink of achievement without actually doing anything: 'Things won are done, joy's soul lies in the doing' (I.ii.279–80). For once you have acted, your act may be confiscated by others, reinscribed in their own contexts and so struck worthless, as easily as Cressida is translated to the Greek camp. What the shattered Troilus finds to say of his unfaithful mistress ('this is, and is not, Cressid') could in fact be said of any word, deed or value, which is always ambiguously yours and not yours, private property and an effect of the Other. Troilus knows that 'the desire is boundless, and the act a slave to limit' (III.ii.), and that such desire breeds 'monstruosity': 'something', any particular action, is nothing, drawn into the past as soon as performed, and only desire, which is lack, is ironically something. This barren history is the narrative *Troilus and Cressida* has to deliver, as both sides struggle to remember what it is they are fighting about, and as, beyond the dramatic conclusion, the war drags on.

I

There is some evidence that the word 'nothing' in Elizabethan English could mean the female genitals.[1] From a phallocentric viewpoint a woman appears to have nothing between her legs, which is as alarming for men as it is reassuring. On the one hand, this apparent lack in the female confirms the male's power over her; on the other hand, it stirs in him unconscious thoughts of his own possible castration, reminding him that his own being may not be as flawlessly complete as he had imagined. The sight of an external lack may stimulate a sense of vacancy within himself, which he can plug, paradoxically, with the woman idealized as fetish: if woman has nothing between her legs then she is a desexualized Madonna, whose purity of being can protect him totemically against the chaos which the female nothing threatens. Desdemona oscillates for Othello between these two impossible roles: 'But I do love thee,' he says of her, 'and when I love thee not/Chaos is come again' (III.ii.92–3). If the female nothing were simple absence, it would pose no problem; but there is in fact no simple absence, since all absence is dependent for its perceptibility upon presence. It is, then, a void which cannot help being powerfully suggestive, a nothing less in the sense of *rien* than of *néant*. The woman's nothing is of a peculiarly convoluted kind, a yawning abyss within which man can lose his virile identity. This modest nothing begins to look like some sublimely terrifying all; and indeed this is the riddle of woman, that though for patriarchy she is in one sense mere deficiency or negation – non-man, defective man – she also has the power to incite the tumultuous 'everything' of desire in man himself, and so to destroy him. How does it come about that this sweet nothing can become a sinister everything?

Paranoid jealousy like Othello's is convinced that a simple nothing – the mistress's lack of infidelity – is, in fact, an abysmal one, a nameless depth beneath the smooth surface of her outward appearance. When Iago cunningly replies 'Nothing' to Othello's request to know what ails him, his comment is ironically exact; but he speculates rightly that Othello will promptly read some dreadful something into this temptingly blank text. This indeed is the classic condition of paranoia, which discerns an oppressively systematic significance in every contingent detail, 'over-reading' the world as Othello over-reads the stolen handkerchief. The closest thing to paranoia, Freud commented dryly, is philosophy; and both are characterized by what he named 'epistemophilia', a pathological obsession with hunting down hidden knowledge, plucking out the heart of a mystery so as to master and possess it. Since there is in fact no heart to the mystery – indeed in *Othello* no mystery at all – this drive for power and knowledge must be endlessly frustrated. Systematically mistrusting appearances, the paranoiac cannot accept that everything lies open to view, that the world just is the way it is with no secret essence, that what he is seeing are not appearances but, amazingly, the real thing.

Sexual jealousy, as readers of Proust will be aware, is fundamentally a crisis of interpretation. Othello insists voyeuristically on seeing, observing, obtaining the 'ocular proof' of his wife's supposed adultery; but the irony of this naive trust in brute fact is that perception is itself a text, requiring interpretation before it means anything at all. And since interpretation is both partial and interminable, 'seeing the facts' is more likely to complicate the issue than to resolve it. Reality itself, things as they are, is thus a kind of blank, needing to be signified before it becomes anything determinate; there is a 'nothing' at the very core of the world, a pervasive absence infiltrating the whole of experience, which can be abolished only by the supplementary benefit of language. The problem, however, is that language itself can be a sort of nothing, as with Iago's insinuating fictions, punching a gaping hole in reality and inducing you to believe in what is not in fact there. For the sexually jealous, the entire world seems struck sickeningly empty of meaning, as it is for Leontes in *The Winter's Tale*:

> Is whispering nothing?
> Is leaning cheek to cheek? Is meeting noses?
> Kissing with inside lip?. . .
> Why, then the world and all that's in't is nothing;
> The covering sky is nothing; Bohemia nothing;
> My wife is nothing; nor nothing have these nothings
> If this be nothing.
>
> (I.ii.284–6, 293–6)

The whole world becomes the female genitals; female sexuality is either in one place – the male's private possession – or it is everywhere.

This, however, is no more than a grossly caricatured version of a problem inherent in ordinary perception. To see anything correctly you need to see more than is actually 'there', since what is there is no more than a pre-linguistic nothing. All interpretation goes beyond its objects; but if it over-reaches them too far it keels over like Othello into an alternative kind of nothing, invoking nameless somethings beneath the surface of life. Othello is on the one hand too literal and gullible a reader, implicitly crediting Iago's lying words; and at the same time too wildly fanciful, fabricating a whole imaginary sub-text at work beneath routine appearances. 'Too little' inverts itself into 'too much'; the man who knows he knows little betrays a pathetic capacity to believe anything. If Othello could 'go beyond' Iago's duplicitous text rather than fall helpless prisoner to its letter then, paradoxically, he would see reality as it is, join signifier and signified together appropriately. Only a certain creative excess of interpretation could restore him to the norm. As it is, he conforms himself obediently to Iago's empty signifiers, filling them with the imaginary signifieds of Desdemona's infidelity.

It is in the nature of paranoid jealousy to overwhelm its object in this way, as a signifier without a referent, a monstrous hermeneutical inflation ('exsufflicate and blown surmises', as Othello calls it in his customary jargon) which feeds off itself without the frailest rooting in reality. Jealousy is a tyrannical language which manipulates the world to suit its own ends, an absolutist law which bends the evidence in its own interests: 'Trifles light as air/Are to the jealous confirmation strong/As proofs of holy writ' (III.iii.326–7). Othello thinks at first that this chain of empty signifiers can be arrested by concrete evidence:

> No, Iago;
> I'll see before I doubt; when I doubt, prove;
> And, on the proof, there is no more but this –
> Away at once with love or jealousy!
>
> (III.iii.193–6)

But since the hypothesis of jealousy rigs the very evidence against which it tests itself, this claim turns out to be purely circular. 'I swear 'tis better to be much abus'd/Than but to know't a little' (III.iii.340–1), Othello cries later – the torment being that to know only something (and who knows more?) is to know that this implies something else of which you are ignorant. Knowledge stretches out to infinity, each present piece of evidence suggesting another which is necessarily absent. Anything definite is thus also unavoidably ambiguous, and sexual jealousy merely intensifies this common state of affairs, reading volumes into a simple handkerchief. 'Freedom', a key term in the play, is ambiguous in this way, since it cannot escape a double denotation of generosity of spirit and sexual promiscuity.

Within the double bind of patriarchy, there is no way in which Desdemona can behave 'properly' towards Cassio without being continually open to the suspicion of behaving 'improperly', no firm borderline between courtesy and lechery. For the woman, to be free is always to be too free; to render an exact, socially dutiful love to Cassio is to risk transgressing the norm. The woman is a constantly travestied text, perpetually open to misreading; she is a stumbling-block in the path of lucid interpretation, unable to be proper without promiscuity, frigid when judicious, never warm without being too hot. As with Cordelia, there is nothing she can do to forestall such misprision, since what she does may always be interpreted to confirm it.

The unpalatable implication of all this is that jealousy is not a form of sexual desire: sexual desire is a form of jealousy. If a woman is capable of being faithful then she is also eternally capable of being unfaithful, just as a word which can be used to speak truth can always be used to deceive. Othello contemplates the possibility of 'nature erring from itself', but this possibility is structural to Nature itself. To desire someone is to see them as an 'other' which one lacks; one cannot speak of desiring that which one possesses. What we desire, then, can never by definition be fully possessed, and the possibility of losing the desired object entirely is thus built into the passion itself. 'Poor and content is rich, and rich enough', Iago remarks, 'But riches fineless is as poor as winter/To him that ever fears he shall be poor' (III.iii.176–8). If to have is to be able to lose, however, then all possession becomes a source of anxiety. This is obvious in the fact that Othello only really comes to desire his wife intensely once he begins to suspect that she is unfaithful to him. His previous 'love' for her is the sheerest narcissism: he wins Desdemona by military boasting, and is agreeably flattered by her admiration for his skill as a professional butcher. To suspect that she is adulterous is to credit her with an identity autonomous of his own, which snaps the narcissistic circuit and begins to undermine his own identity. Much of his jealousy is no more than this self-regarding fear that his own magnificently replete selfhood is collapsing from the inside, as the female nothing, the green girl who gasped at his tall tales, becomes a sinisterly independent something. But if such lack and autonomy are logical to all desire, then all desire is a kind of monstrosity or perversion. Woman is that which man can never possess, that which eludes his mastery and so breeds in him a feverish activity of 'over-interpretation'. Inflated signifiers, slanderous misreadings, infinite webs of text and tortuous *aporias* ('I think my wife be honest, and I think she is not') would seem to go 'naturally' with erotic love. It is in the nature of such Eros to override the measure, generate delusion, squint at its object. *Othello* is not a play about sexual deviancy, but about the deviancy of sex.

This is not, however, to justify the cynicism of an Iago. If Othello in the end is unable to distinguish between delusion and reality, Iago has severed them too rigorously all along. 'I am not what I am' signals not a crisis of identity but a smug self-affirmation: Iago is the exact opposite of whatever he appears to be, which is a consistent enough way of possessing oneself. Appearances for Iago are just empty rituals to be pragmatically manipulated: 'I must show out a flag and sign of love,/Which is indeed but sign' (I.i.157–8). But nothing for Shakespeare is *but* sign: the signifier is always active in respect of its meaning, not some hollow container to be discarded at will. Iago is one of a long line of possessive individualists in Shakespeare who locate reality only in bodily appetite, believing that they can exploit signs and forms from the outside while remaining themselves unscathed by the consequent mystification. Whereas Othello lives straight out of an imaginary self-image, his very being indissociable from rhetoric and theatricality, Iago scorns such burnished discourse as 'mere prattle, without practice'. But both Othello's histrionic 'bombast' and Iago's brisk materialism miss the measure. Othello starts off with a wholly 'imaginary' relation to reality: his rotund, mouth-filling rhetoric signifies a delusory completeness of being, in which the whole world becomes a signified obediently reflecting back the imperious signifier of the self. Even Desdemona becomes his 'fair warrior', as though he can grasp nothing which he has not first translated into his own military idiom. From this deceptively secure standpoint, Othello is then pitched violently into the 'symbolic order' of desire, where signifier and signified never quite coincide. The problem, then, is how to recognize, unlike the cynically naturalistic Iago, that signs and illusions are structural to reality – that all experience, because driven by desire, has an inescapable dimension of fantasy and mystification – without falling prey to the tragic lunacy of an Othello, for whom appearance and reality come to merge into a seamless whole. Iago fails to see that all bodily appetite is caught up in discourse and symbolism, which are not 'superstructural' pieties but part of its inward form. Othello knows this too well, and comes to mistake the sign for the reality. How does one distinguish between taking appearances for reality, and acknowledging the reality of appearances? Failing to make such a distinction, *Othello* suggests, is a psychopathological condition; but it also suggests, more alarmingly, that this psychopathology may be intrinsic to everyday life.

II

If *Othello* portrays a man in hot pursuit of nothing, *Hamlet* reverses the perspective and tells the story from the standpoint of that nothing itself. It is as though the experiment here is to put 'nothing' at the structural centre of the text, making it the subject rather than the object of the action. The mysterious opacity of *Othello*, the central recalcitrance which baffles and resists interpretation, is none other than woman and desire.[2] In *Hamlet* that opacity, while closely related to female sexuality, is quite evidently the protagonist himself, whose enigmatic being is legendary in world literature. The particular form of negativity which

Hamlet experiences is melancholia, which, rather like paranoid jealousy, drains the world of value and dissolves it into nauseating nothingness:

> O, that this too too solid flesh would melt,
> Thaw, and resolve itself into a dew!
> Or that the Everlasting had not fix'd
> His canon 'gainst self-slaughter! O God! God!
> How weary, stale, flat, and unprofitable,
> Seem to me all the uses of this world!
>
> (I.ii.129–34)

Melancholy, as we have seen in *The Merchant of Venice*, levels all values, renders the odds even, and makes all bits of the world banally interchangeable. All experiences become exactly equivalent in their triviality. For Freud, melancholy involves a diminution of the ego not far from Othello's steady collapse of self: the ego identifies itself with a lost object of love, and this pervasive lack gradually overwhelms it. What Hamlet has importantly lost appears to be less his father than his mother, who has committed at least two grievous errors: she has revealed herself capable of desire, a scandalous thing in a woman, let alone in a mother; and that desire is not for Hamlet himself, but for another man.

Once the imaginary relation between Hamlet and Gertrude has been ruptured by the entry of Claudius, Hamlet loiters hesitantly on the brink of the 'symbolic order' (the system of allotted sexual and social roles in society), unable and unwilling to take up a determinate position within it. Indeed he spends most of his time eluding whatever social and sexual positions society offers him, whether as chivalric lover, obedient revenger or future king. As fluid as his father's ghost and as fast-talking as any Shakespearian clown, Hamlet riddles and bamboozles his way out of being definitively known, switching masks and sliding the signifier to protect his inner privacy of being against the power and knowledge of the court. This inner being, as he coldly informs Gertrude, evades the mark of the signifier:

> 'Tis not alone my inky cloak, good mother,
> Nor customary suits of solemn black,
> Nor windy suspiration of forc'd breath,
> No, nor the fruitful river in the eye,
> Nor the dejected haviour of the visage,
> Together with all forms, moods, shapes of grief,
> That can denote me truly. These, indeed, seem;
> For they are actions that a man might play;
> But I have that within which passes show —
> These but the trappings and the suits of woe.
>
> (I.ii.77–86)

Later, he will be scandalized that Rosencrantz and Guildenstern, slow-witted lackeys of the state, should presume to penetrate his inward essence, pluck out the heart of his mystery. But the irony of this, as in *Othello*, is that there is no heart of the mystery to be plucked out. Hamlet has no 'essence' of being whatsoever, no inner sanctum to be safeguarded: he is pure deferral and diffusion, a hollow void which offers nothing determinate to be known. His 'self' consists simply in the range of gestures with which he resists available definitions, not in a radical alternative beyond their reach. It is thus wholly parasitic on the positions it refuses: like Iago he is not what he is, but whereas for Iago this means preserving a secret identity apart from public show, Hamlet's jealous sense of unique selfhood is no more than the negation of anything in particular. How could it be otherwise, when he rejects the signifiers by which alone the self, as signified, comes into its determinacy? That latter-day Hamlet, J. Alfred Prufrock, believes himself in possession of an 'overwhelming question', perhaps the key to the riddle of the universe, which sets him sharply apart from his socially conformist acquaintances. But does Prufrock really have such an insight, the problem being one of adequately articulating it, or does the fact that the question refuses all articulation suggest that it is an hallucination, the mere ghost of a question, a portentous nothing or signified without a signifier? Hamlet, the superfluous man, is sheer empty excess over the given, a being radically incommensurate with any other, and so the ruin of all metaphor and exchange. Indeed, he spends almost the whole play refusing to practise such an exchange (take Claudius's life in revenge for his father's), and at one point casts doubt upon that entire logic: 'use every man after his desert, and who shall scape whipping?'

It is clear from all this that the 'character' of Hamlet would not be the most secure foundation on which to construct a political order. The political future lies not with him but with Coriolanus. Coriolanus, though literally a patrician, is perhaps Shakespeare's most developed study of a bourgeois individualist, those 'new men' (for the most part villains in Shakespeare) who live 'As if a man were author of himself/And knew no other kin' (V.iii.36–7). Ruthlessly self-consistent and self-identical, Coriolanus is as superbly assured in his inward being as Hamlet is shattered in his. For him, as for Iago, the signifier of public forms is to be scorned. Why should he be ceremonially exhibited to the people, crave their assent to his name and title, when he is perfectly well aware of who he is? Like the possessive individualist Achilles, Coriolanus confers value and meaning on himself in fine disregard for social opinion, acting as signifier and signified together; he is a particularly blatant disproval of Polonius's pious belief that being true to oneself entails fidelity to others. (Polonius's advice in any case assumes that 'truth to self' is a coherent notion, which the play certainly does not.) Whereas Hamlet falls apart in the space between himself and his actions, Coriolanus is nothing *but* his actions, a circular, blindly persistent process of self-definition. He cannot imagine what it would be like not to be himself, as Hamlet cannot imagine what it would be like to be anybody in particular. Both men are thus a kind of nothing – Hamlet because he is never identical with himself, Coriolanus because he is exactly what he is, and so a sort of blank tautology. Neither will engage in reciprocal exchange or submit to the signifier: Coriolanus 'forbad all names;/He was a kind of nothing, titleless,/Till he had forg'd himself a name i' th' fire/Of burning Rome' (V.i.13–15). But the paradox of such private enterprise of the self is that although it regards personal identity as private, autonomous and non-exchangeable, it is historically bound up with the full-blown exchange economy of commodity production. What gets exchanged in this form of society are material goods, which become 'social' at the point where their owners are made private. The reciprocity of commodity exchange stands in, so to speak, for the relational bonds between persons; and though Shakespeare's work is far from admiring this condition, it does at least lay the basis for a kind of social 'order', as Hamlet clearly does not. Coriolanus may come to grief in his play, but considered as a bourgeois prototype rather than Roman patrician there is nothing historically necessary about his death. On the contrary, he prefigures the time – not far off from Shakespeare's England – when a whole society will fall prey to the ideology of self-authorship, when all individuals will be only begetters of themselves, private entrepreneurs of their bodies and sole proprietors of a labour force. The tragedy of Hamlet, by contrast, is in some sense historically necessary: it would be highly embarrassing to have a man like this hanging around Fortinbras's court.

Hamlet's reluctance or inability to enter the symbolic order, and his revulsion from the sexuality which reproduces it, are in one sense regressive states of being. His attachment to his mother fragments his being into an unfulfillable desire which, since it swerves round all determinate objects (Ophelia, filial duty, political power) cannot be represented other than as a lack. But this psychological regression is also, paradoxically, a kind of social progressiveness. Hamlet is a radically transitional figure, strung out between a traditional social order to which he is marginal, and a future epoch of achieved bourgeois individualism which will surpass it.[3] But because of this we can glimpse in him a negative critique of the forms of subjectivity typical of *both* these regimes. It is his regressiveness which makes him so modern: eccentric to traditional order but still oppressed by it, unable to transgress its definitive limits into a fully alternative style of being, the resultant 'decentring' of his identity satirically questions the violent closure of bourgeois individualism as much as that of Claudius's court. In this sense, Hamlet is even more proleptic than Coriolanus, looking forward to a time (our own?) when that individualist conception of the self will itself enter into crisis. This is why many commentators have discerned something peculiarly 'modernist' in Hamlet – not that he is a twentieth-century existentialist intellectual in Jacobean clothing, but because he stands at the tentative beginnings of a history which may now, at least in some of its aspects, be drawing to a close. Although he is a deeply 'subjective' figure, and experiences that subjectivity as a crippling burden, it has not yet been disciplined and 'naturalized' into the oppressive unity which will later convert consciousness itself into a kind of prison. What it is to be a subject, in short, is a political problem for Hamlet, as it has once more become a political problem for us. Hamlet signifies the beginnings of the dissolution of the old feudalist subject, who is as yet, however, unable to name himself affirmatively in any other way. If we too are as yet unable to give a name to a different form of subjectivity, it is for the opposite reason – that we, unlike Hamlet, are the end-products of a history of bourgeois individualism beyond which we can only gropingly feel our way. Whatever the difference, this may be one reason why the (non-)character of Hamlet seems to speak to us more urgently than any other of Shakespeare's tragic protagonists.

5   Value: *King Lear, Timon of Athens, Antony and Cleopatra*

King Lear opens with a bout of severe linguistic inflation, as Goneril and Regan rival each other in lying rhetoric. Goneril pitches her love for Lear beyond all language and value, and so ironically reveals this 'more than all' as just the resounding nothing that it is:

> Sir, I love you more than word can wield the matter;
> Dearer than eyesight, space, and liberty;
> Beyond what can be valued, rich or rare;
> No less than life, with grace, health, beauty, honour;
> As much as child e'er lov'd, or father found;
> A love that makes breath poor and speech unable;
> Beyond all manner of so much I love you.
>
> (I.i.54–60)

Goneril's love for Lear is indeed beyond value, since it doesn't exist; it is inarticulable not because it transcends meaning but because it has none. By representing her love as the negation of any particular object, she merely succeeds in cancelling it out, just as she uses language only to suggest its utter inadequacy. Goneril, whom Albany will later call 'Thou worse than any name' (V.iii.156), fails to see that definitions can be creative as well as restrictive, fashioning something from nothing. It is then up to Regan to negate her sister's negativity to imply an even more grandiose all, claiming, contradictorily, that Goneril has both defined her own love precisely and fallen woefully short.

Within this stage-managed charade, where 'all' has been so radically devalued, Cordelia's murmured 'Nothing' is the only sound currency. Cordelia is characteristically exact to maintain that she can say nothing to outdo her sisters, for who can trump 'all'? Lear warns her that nothing will come of this – 'Nothing will come of nothing. Speak again' (I.i.89) – but as usual he is mistaken: when meaning has been inflated beyond measure, nothing *but* nothing, a drastic reduction of signs to cyphers, will be enough to restabilize the verbal coinage. Only by a fundamental inversion and undercutting of this whole lunatic language game can the ground be cleared for a modest 'something' to begin gradually to emerge. That 'something' is in fact already figured in Cordelia's reply. With scrupulous precision, she informs Lear that she loves him 'According to my bond; no more nor less' (I.i.92), appealing away from the crazed subjectivism of the King's whimsical demand for love to the web of impersonal constraints and obligations of kinship. The other side of reckless inflation is the crass utilitarian exactitude with which Lear believes human love can be quantified; Cordelia counters the first with a more authentic precision, and the second, later in the play, with a forgiveness which is creative excess. Lear himself, of course, cannot see such precision as anything but paucity of spirit, gripped as he is by a semiotic crisis which spurs him to shed the substance of power while retaining 'The name, and all th'addition to a king', voiding the referent while clutching at the empty signifier. He trusts to the aura of a title, even as he credits lines drawn on a piece of paper: 'Of all these bounds, even from this line to this . . . We make thee lady.' No map can fully represent the terrain it signifies, just as Lear has struck his own title abstract, divorced it from material life.

Lear's paranoid drama, like the Malvolio-taunting scene

of *Twelfth Night*, fashions a verbal nexus to which there is no 'outside', double-binding Cordelia so that to play her role or refuse it, speak or keep silent, become equally falsifying. (The Fool will later complain that he is whipped whether he speaks truth, lies or holds his peace.) France's gratuitous action of accepting Cordelia even when 'her price is fallen' makes something of nothing, cutting across Lear's world of precisely calculated imprecisions, but he can extricate Cordelia from the charade only in a way which that fiction can nullify as beggarly sentimentalism. When social reality has become mystified to its core, truth can lie only beyond its boundaries, as France lies beyond the extreme limit of Britain (Dover cliff). But such truth can therefore also be neutralized as marginal aberration. Cordelia consequently disappears into the future of the play, and truth becomes a simple inversion of whatever Lear affirms: Cordelia, France comments, is 'most rich, being poor', just as Kent finds that 'Freedom lies hence, and banishment is here'. We shall see later that the truth of a false condition can be articulated only in the discourse of madness, in a language which raises political insanity to the second power, parodying and redoubling it so as to deconstruct it from the inside. There can be no straight talking, no bold gesture of unmasking, which will not be absorbed and reinflected by the nexus of delusion, becoming yet another mask and falsehood in its turn; only the coupling of two negatives can hope to produce a positive.

In severing himself from Cordelia, spokeswoman for the material bonds of kinship, Lear cuts himself off from his own physical life, leaving his consciousness to consume itself in a void. In madness, as in sleepwalking, the mind ranges impotently beyond the body's limits, capable of destroying its substance: Edgar declares that he eats poisonous matter when seized by devils. Lear's mind is so tormented by his daughters' cruelty that his body is impervious to the storm which assails it: '. . . When the mind's free/The body's delicate; this tempest in my mind/ Doth from my senses take all feeling else,/Save what beats

there' (III.iv.11–14). Body and consciousness, once dis-
jointed, are each reduced to a kind of nothing: the former
becomes an insentient blank, the latter, unmoulded by
material constraint, emptily devours itself. Gloucester,
confronted with Lear's agony, yearns to unhinge his own
mind and body:

> The King is mad; how stiff is my vile sense,
> That I stand up, and have ingenious feeling
> Of my huge sorrows! Better I were distract;
> So should my thoughts be sever'd from my griefs,
> And woes by wrong imaginations lose
> The knowledge of themselves.

(IV.vi.279–84)

What Gloucester will finally learn, once blindness has
thrust the brute fact of his body into consciousness, is not to
give the body the slip but to 'see feelingly', to allow sight
(the symbol of a potentially unbridled self) to be constrained
from within by the compassionate senses. Gloucester's
body becomes his mode of communication with the
material world (he 'smell[s] his way to Dover'), more
solidly reliable than the verbal trickery of his bastard son.
At the extreme outer limit of political society – on Dover
cliff – those fictions can be induced by the fruitfully
deceitful ministrations of Edgar to keel over into a kind of
truth. This painful rediscovery of the body is what Lear
must also learn. To regain touch with the harsh materiality
of things, to discover that one is nothing in comparison with
all one had imagined, is in that very act to become
something:

> To say 'ay' and 'no' to everything that I said! 'Ay' and
> 'no' too was no good divinity. When the rain came to
> wet me once, and the wind to make me chatter; when
> the thunder would not peace at my bidding; there I
> found 'em, there I smelt 'em out. Go to, they are not
> men of their words. They told me I was everything;
> 'tis a lie – I am not ague-proof.

(IV.vi.)

To say 'ay' and 'no' to everything is to say nothing; Lear has 'smelt out' this truth, absorbed it through the stuff of the ambivalently linking, limiting body, whose stringent boundaries the storm has thrown into exposure. To know your own nothingness is to become something, as the Fool is wiser than fools because he knows his own folly and so can see through theirs.

To be purely bodily, like the non-linguistic animals, is to be essentially passive, a prey to the biological determinations of one's nature. Goneril and Regan, despite a ruthless activism which springs from being unbounded by sensuous compassion, are fundamentally passive in this sense, unable after their initial dissembling to falsify what they are. In this sense they are the true sisters of Cordelia, who is likewise unswervingly faithful to her own being. Edmund sees himself as equally fixed by nature ('I should have been that I am, had the maidenliest star in the firmament twinkled on my bastardizing' (I.ii)), but by reflecting sardonically on his own determinants he is able to escape a blind enslavement to them. He is a self-creating opportunist who can manipulate others' appetites to his own advantage precisely because he knows his own so well. Like Iago, he moves primarily at the level of mystifying language, hostile to physical affinities, intent on rupturing the relations between his father and brother. By consciously appropriating what one ineluctably is, it is possible in part to transcend limit; and this is also true of Edgar and Kent, who deliberately embrace the wretchedness and delusion through which Lear is blindly forced, submitting to degrading limit in order finally to surpass it. The play seeks to distinguish the creative passivity of being constrained in the flesh by the needs of others, from the destructive passivity of being a mere function of one's appetites. For consciousness to be wholly bound by the body is to be a bestial slave to limit; to be purely active, however, is to over-reach those physical bonds for the vacuous freedom of an exploitative individualism. Both modes of being are a kind of nothing, and 'something' emerges in the play only elusively, glimpsed fitfully in the dialectic between them. The paradox which *King Lear* explores is that it is 'natural' for the human animal to transcend its own limits, yet this creative tendency to exceed oneself is also the source of destructiveness. Being 'untrue' to their own nature is natural to human beings: what we call culture or history is an open-ended transformation of fixed boundaries, a transcendence of mere appetite or rich surplus over precise measure. But when this process transgresses the body's confines too far, it violates the bonds of sensuous compassion and begins to prey on physical life itself. A hubristic, overweening consciousness must then be called sharply to order, shrunk back violently within the cramped frontiers of creaturely existence. The problem is how to do this without extinguishing that authentic self-exceeding which distinguishes an animal with history from other natural species.

One can pinpoint this difficult dialectic as the problem of respecting a norm or measure while simultaneously going beyond it. Excess may swamp such measure with its own too much, toppling over by a curious logic into less than anything; yet such superfluity is also precisely that which marks off men and women from the inhuman precision of beasts, or indeed of Goneril and Regan. The sisters fail to understand why their father should require a retinue of knights, and looking at Lear's gang of macho ruffians one can see their point. Lear's reply, however, is telling:

> O, reason not the need! Our basest beggars
> Are in the poorest thing superfluous.
> Allow not nature more than nature needs,
> Man's life is cheap as beast's.

> (II.iv.263–6)

There is no *reason* why human beings should delight in more than is strictly necessary for their physical survival; it is just structural to the human animal that demand should outstrip exact need, that culture should be of its nature. It is this capacity for a certain lavish infringement of exact

limit which distinguishes humankind, just as the play's first
scene reveals the same capacity to lie at the source of what
makes humans immeasurably more destructive than any
other species. Surplus is radically ambivalent, not least in
economic life. Too many material possessions blunt one's
capacity for fellow feeling, swaddling one's senses from
exposure to the misery of others. If one could truly *feel* that
wretchedness, register it sharply on the senses, then one
would be moved to share one's surplus with the poor in a
fundamental, irreversible redistribution of wealth:

> Take physic, pomp;
> Expose thyself to feel what wretches feel,
> That thou mayst shake the superflux to them,
> And show the heavens more just. . .

> (III.iv.34–7)

> Let the superfluous and lust-dieted man
> That slaves your ordinance, that will not see
> Because he does not feel, feel your power quickly;
> So distribution should undo excess,
> And each man have enough.

> (IV.i.68–72)

Against this image of a destructive surplus is balanced
Cordelia's forgiveness of her father, a gratuitous excess of
the strict requirements of justice. It is a kind of nothing, a
refusal to calculate debt, out of which something may come.

What is superfluous or excessive about human beings,
King Lear suggests, is nothing less than language itself,
which constantly outruns the confines of the body. 'The
worse is not,' declares Edgar, 'So long as we can say "This
is the worst" ' (IV.i.28–9). By naming an ultimate limit,
speech transcends it in that very act, undoing its own
pronouncement by its own performance. Language is the
edge we have over biology, but it is a mixed blessing.
Goneril and Regan's speech is rigorously exact, pared to
the purely functional: Goneril tells Edmund to 'spare
speech' when she uses him as a messenger. The disguised

Kent's language is as parodically plain as Edgar's is elaborately confusing; Oswald's foppish idiom incites Kent (whose reports are said to be 'nor more nor clipp'd, but so') to spurn him as an 'unnecessary letter'. Language, like much else in the play, has a problem in pitching itself at the elusive point between too much and too little – except, perhaps, in the formally precise yet generously affectionate discourse of Cordelia. Cordelia blends largesse and limitation on her first appearance in the play, when she reminds Lear that her love, though freely given, must be properly divided between himself and her future husband; and the same balance is present in her combination of physical rootedness and freedom of spirit. In this sense, she symbolically resolves many of the play's formal antinomies.

The only problem, however, is that she dies. Edgar's closing injuction – 'Speak what we feel, not what we ought to say' – is no trite tag,[1] denoting as it does that organic unity of body and language, that shaping of signs by the senses, of which Cordelia is representative; but the play has also demonstrated that to speak what one feels is no easy business. For if it is structural to human nature to surpass itself, and if language is the very index and medium of this, then there would seem a contradiction at the very core of the linguistic animal which makes it 'natural' for signs to come adrift from things, consciousness to overstep physical bonds, values to get out of hand and norms to be destructively overridden. It is not, after all, simply a matter of reconciling fixed opposites: it is a matter of regulating what would seem an ineradicable contradiction in the material structure of the human creature. *King Lear* is a tragedy because it stares this contradiction full in the face, aware that no poetic symbolism is adequate to resolve it.

II

An obsession with strict exchanges is typical of middle-class utilitarianism; the aristocracy are traditionally more spendthrift. This is certainly true of Timon of Athens, one of the last of Shakespeare's big spenders, whose grotesque generosity to his friends is a subtle form of egotism, triumphantly trumping their own gifts by returning them many-fold. Timon's giving is a way of cancelling and forestalling the bountifulness of others; since he refuses to learn how to receive, he does not know what a genuine gift is. The act of giving is for Timon its own aesthetic thrill; a man who will bestow anything on anybody is as superbly indifferent to particular persons and use values as the most mean-spirited miser. There is a ruthless formalism and abstraction about Timon's big-heartedness which overrides intrinsic merits, scattering his surplus indiscriminately as the fancy takes him. His munificence is thus rather like money itself, perturbing all particular values in its restless expansiveness. As the Poet says of his own unbridled imagination:

> My free drift
> Halts not particularly, but moves itself
> In a wide sea of tax.

> (I.i.48–50)

This gratuitous generosity turns out to be literally self-destructive, as Timon sinks deeper into debt; and the snarling misanthropy which then overtakes him is merely an inverted image of his erstwhile beneficence. To condemn all individuals indiscriminately is just as abstract as to reward them all indifferently. 'All' and 'nothing' turn out once more to be bedfellows rather than antagonists. It is not fortuitous (though some scholars have found it so) that the play should interpolate into its main narrative an apparently unrelated sub-plot centred on Alcibiades' plea for mercy from the Senate for a friend who has killed in hot blood. It is logical that Timon's prodigality should remind Shakespeare of the issues of mercy and justice, measure for measure. The Senate are as formalistic in their insistence that Alcibiades' friend must die as Timon is in his whimsical patronage; the law, as we have seen already, is coolly indifferent to particular individuals, and thus ironically apes Timon's supposed generosity. In contrast to such abstract formalism, mercy draws attention to specific mitigating factors, and Alcibiades acknowledges that these must temper rather than set aside the claims of justice:

> To kill, I grant, is sin's extremest gust;
> But in defence, by mercy, 'tis most just.
> To be in anger is impiety;
> But who is man that is not angry?
> Weigh but the crime with this.
>
> (III.v.54–8)

The Senate, however, are not impressed, and Alcibiades is banished for his pains, if not for his atrocious verse.

If Timon of Athens does not exactly engage our heartfelt sympathies, Shakespeare's other two aristocratic big spenders, Antony and Cleopatra, are rather more successful. Perhaps the most revealing approach to this play is through the work of W. B. Yeats. Yeats was the self-appointed spokesman of a decaying aristocracy, the Anglo-Irish Ascendency, who sentimentalized the Irish peasantry they exploited; and his apologia for their passing took the form of swaggering defiance, a reckless celebration of heroic vitality against the niggardly calculations of the middle classes. If the aristocracy are on their way out, then they might as well pass away with a bang rather than a whimper, dancing demonically on the edge of their own grave, squandering their energies in proud disdain for petty-bourgeois prudence, and so dying as they have lived. Confronted with imminent death, the aristocracy make an heroic virtue out of sordid necessity; Yeats gathers the tragedy of their decline into the aesthetic artifice of eternity, rejoicing with fine Nietzschean bravado in the teeth of the historically inevitable. Loss becomes gain, the nadir transfigured to the acme, corruption translated to a triumphant artefact. In this aristocratic or *Übermensch* ethic, each individual becomes his or her own autonomous measure, self-generating and self-delighting, not to be compared with others or subdued to a mean. Thom Gunn's poem 'Lerici', also about a profligate aristocrat, puts the point well:

> Byron was worth the sea's pursuit: his touch
> Was masterful to water, audience
> To which he could react until an end.
> Strong swimmers, fishermen, explorers: such
> Dignify death by fruitless violence,
> Squandering all their little left to spend.

If this violent self-expenditure is to be authentic, however, it must keep one cold eye on its own historical hoplessness. The carefree aristocratic affirmation is shot through with a lacerating death-wish, as its own desperate futility continually offers to undermine it.

It is this Nietzschean or Yeatsian ethic which informs *Antony and Cleopatra*, a play which opens with the censorious remark that Antony's dotage 'o'erflows the measure'. The desperate gamble of the Egyptian world is that if you can only overflow the measure extravagantly enough, then you might just struggle free of its calibrating tyranny into a new transcendence. A wild, wilful self-lavishing ('There's beggary in the love that can be reckon'd') may undercut the mean radically enough to transfigure it, so that Antony and Cleopatra can become their own unique norm, a new creation incommensurable with anything beyond themselves. To be utterly dissolute and undone may, by a strange logic, invert itself into victory (Yeats's 'tragic joy'); and the play is full of such dialectical images of processes which, when pressed to their extreme, tip over into their opposites. The relationship of Antony and Cleopatra makes one little room an everywhere, becoming the sole yardstick by which an otherwise blankly senseless world takes on meaning ; the stringent proportions of utilitarian Rome are rejected for a quite different scale of value, linked to intensity and superabundance. Cleopatra is the 'lass unparalleled' who 'beggars all description'; Antony's poker-faced description of a crocodile to the thick-witted Ledipus plays on a thing's incapacity to be defined as anything but itself:

> It is shap'd, sir, like itself, and it is as broad as it has breadth; it is just so high as it is, and moves with its own organs. It lives by that which nourisheth it, and the elements once out of it, it transmigrates.
>
> (II.vii.)

As with the subjectivist Trojans of *Troilus and Cressida*, no object is inherently valuable, and there are thus no rational grounds on which to choose between them. Antony's rash decision to fight by sea rather than by land is in the classic existentialist sense an *acte gratuit*, performed defiantly for its own sake. It is an effective way of speeding on the death in which all odds will be even.

The play, then, seizes one term of Shakespeare's customary contradiction – surplus, excess – and rather than seeking to reconcile it with its contrary (equitable exchange), lives it with such fanatical intensity that a perverse kind of value is wrested from this very violent disproportioning. What is known as partial and one-sided takes itself as ultimate, in an ambiguously fertile and lethal fiction. This resolute living towards death, which crams each empty moment of time with hectic pleasure, and transforms each passing sensation into an ecstatic work of art, is the last word in political irresponsibility, and knows itself to be such. In *Antony and Cleopatra* the traditionalist social order flamboyantly burns itself out, rots itself with motion, snatching a final arrogant victory from its own demise. Creative abundance and clogging superfluity become well-nigh impossible to distinguish. Unfit for social order, Antony and Cleopatra illuminate the meagre pragmatism of calculating Rome in the fire of their self-immolation. What the play's stonily realist characters have to say of the ageing lecher Antony and his shrewish strumpet Cleopatra is at once to the point and gloriously irrelevant; the language of politics no longer meshes with the discourse of value, and the play simply dramatizes their

contradiction, practises what Brecht called 'complex
seeing', without seeking to resolve it. Banished from the
political arena, creative superfluity has now pushed free
into a dimension of its own, become its own self-delighting
principle quite sundered from history. This poetic transcendence is at the same time the measure of its defeat.

What deconstructs political order in the play is desire,
and the figure for this is Cleopatra. In predictably
patriarchal style, Cleopatra is portrayed as capricious and
self-contradictory, undoing all coherence in her exasperating
inconsistency. She is, as it were, pure heterogeneity, an
'infinite variety' which eludes any stable position. Less a
rounded 'character' than a complex flow of impulse, her joy
in the inconsequential mocks Octavius's views of 'centrality', embodying a 'feminine' trust to sensuous experience
which threatens to subvert the public world. Both fearful
and admiring of this quality, the play seeks to contain it by
making Cleopatra at the same time an image of Nature. If
woman for patriarchy is guileful artifice (Cleopatra is a
consummate actress), she is also, contradictorily, purely
natural. It is as though Cleopatra has the amplitude and
spontaneity of Nature itself, containing all things within
herself (everything 'becomes' her), as Nature houses an
infinite variety of contrary impulses. If she has no fixed
identity in herself, she is nevertheless the space within
which all creation renews itself, in which conflicting moods
converge ('to chide, to laugh, to weep') and every passion
strives to make itself 'fair and admir'd'. Her disruptive
'feminine' fickleness can thus be offset by a sense that she
harmonizes multitudes in her own being. The effect of this
is to blur the borderline between the most 'unnatural'
whimsy, intrigue and affectation, and the inexhaustible
variety and mutability of Nature itself, just as Enobarbus's
great hymn of praise to her ('The barge she sat in, like a
burnish'd throne . . .') subtly deconstructs the distinction
between Nature and culture, dissolving both into an all-
encompassing Eros. If the woman figures a politically
subversive desire, she can also come to symbolize, like

Nature itself, the great pre-political matrix from which all cultures proceed, and which supposedly transcends their petty particularities. Woman would appear in this sense to be on the side of both anarchy and order, though the order she symbolizes runs 'deeper' than the political.

If Cleopatra transmutes all things into her own substance, changing one quality into another ('vilest things/ Become themselves in her'), then she is uneasily reminiscent of those potentially anarchic forces we have seen at work elsewhere in Shakespeare. Yet to be the space where all things are commutable is to be a kind of cohering principle, even if of a dangerously levelling kind, and so can be presented as an image of variety within order. The chief name for this in Shakespeare is Nature, to which he will finally turn for a mystifying 'resolution' of the historical problems which beset him.

6 Nature: *As You Like It, The Winter's Tale, The Tempest*

Both *King Lear* and *Timon of Athens* consider, only to reject, the doctrine of primitivism, that is to say, an idealization of human beings in their 'natural' state, free from the corruption of civilization. Against this sentimental myth, both plays recognize that culture is 'natural' to human beings, that however many civilized lendings you cast off you will never strip down to the bare forked creature man, since this simple pre-cultural being is itself a cultural fiction. What you will always find is a linguistic animal, one whose nature contains the power to go beyond itself. Lear's body/clothes metaphor is a grossly simplistic image of the relations between Nature and culture, as the play itself recognizes. Instead, Shakespeare deconstructs this binary opposition, showing how each term inheres in the other; and his first major essay in this mode is *As You Like It*. This play shows well enough how Nature and artifice are allies as well as enemies, not least when it comes to that ambivalently spontaneous and factitious emotion, erotic love. At one point in the play, the disguised Rosalind plays herself to her lover, Orlando; but then every self-presentation is for Shakespeare a kind of play-acting, every process of natural development, as in Jaques's great speech on the ages of man, presentable in theatrical terms. To view Nature as awesomely 'other' is just as ideological in this work as to treat it as a moral text in which one can trace, narcissistically, one's own subjective moods. Touchstone, one of 'nature's naturals' (a Fool), pines for the court; the rustic lovers speak with rhetorical artifice; Jaques's jaded satire of civilization is itself a piece of civilized self-indulgence. We cannot speak of a simple antithesis of country and city in a society where, as Corin the shepherd knows, commercial values are penetrating and dislocating the rural economy itself.[1]

It is just this deconstruction of the court/country polarity which will provide Shakespeare in the last comedies with a kind of resolution to the problems we have pursued throughout his work. The crux of this resolution can be found in the exchange between Polixenes and Perdita on art and Nature in *The Winter's Tale*:

Perdita	For I have heard it said
	There is an art which in their piedness shares
	With great creating nature.
Polixenes	Say there be.
	Yet nature is made better by no mean
	But nature makes that mean; so over that art,
	Which you say adds to nature, is an art
	That nature makes. You see, sweet maid, we marry
	A gentler scion to the wildest stock,
	And make conceive a bark of baser kind
	By bud of nobler race. This is an art
	Which does mend nature – change it rather; but
	The art itself is nature.

(IV.iv.87–97)

Nature itself produces the means of its own transformation, contains that which goes beyond it. What goes beyond it – art, civilization, culture, language, love – is thus no mere external 'supplement' to it, but is internal to its very design. If Nature is always cultural, then a particular culture can always be seen as natural. Those forms of surplus are legitimate which have their roots in the very natural order they transcend, and which provides the source of that transcendence. The play's own name for this is Perdita herself, the gentler scion wedded to the wildest stock. Aristocrats transcend the common herd but are themselves ultimately products of Nature, and being grafted on to it can bring it to perfection. There is a fundamental natural equality between all human beings despite their social rank ('The self-same sun that shines upon his court/Hides not his visage from our cottage, but/Looks on alike' (IV.iv.436–8)), yet this shared nature is refined by civilized breeding beyond itself, generating hierarchial differences which none the less retain roots in a common soil. The social relations between persons thus have the paradoxical structure of metaphor: individuals are both the same, and different. At the fundamental level of Nature, as of justice and mercy, they must all be regarded as equal; but this general structure must not be allowed to erode particular distinctions. These distinctions of class and rank are themselves natural, because somehow produced by Nature; for Nature is at once an amorphous, indivisible process and a structure of precise discriminations. The point of Perdita's stunning speech about flowers is to show Nature as both profuse and particular: it is a fluid, diverse, inexhaustible energy but also a given structure of intrinsic values. It thus allows Shakespeare to image a kind of ceaseless heterogeneity which will not be disruptive; and it also provides him with a figure of common humanity less alarmingly reified than the law, since if nothing could be more pervasively general than Nature, nothing could be more earthy and immediate either.

The concept of Nature also reconciles common and private ownership. For everyone belongs to Nature, and so belongs to each other; yet the last comedies make much of the father–child relationship as a paradigm of authentic individual possession. My children are in one sense mine only by derivation from Nature, yet they are also my inalienable products, stamped with my life and labour, in which I find myself precisely mirrored. Private property is thus naturalized along with the aristocracy. The discourse whose task is to naturalize a particular social order, imbuing it with the immutability and inevitability of Nature itself, is commonly termed ideology; and the last comedies are therefore ideological in a very precise meaning of that term.

It is worth noting that Shakespeare's 'resolution' of his dilemmas depends upon a logical slide in the meaning of the word 'Nature'. For to say that Nature produces the means of its own transfiguration is simply to say, trivially, that everything in the world springs from the stuff of the world. It does not necessarily imply that art and culture are therefore 'natural' in a value-laden sense of the term; that is to say, to be morally desired as conducive to human welfare. Nuclear weapons are natural in the one sense but not in the other. The 'resolutions' of the late comedies thus rest not only upon a reactionary mystification of Nature but on a logical mistake. If Nature always already contains its own surplus, then it presumably contains as part of its norm that transformation of the given which is murder, as much as the various 'creative' transcendences we have examined. What Nature would seem precisely not to supply is the criteria by which you might distinguish between positive and negative forms of 'excess'.

The reconciliation of Nature and culture is, inseparably, a uniting of the body and language. For the body, however much a social product, is also a biological given, and language is Shakespeare's primary symbol of the culture which surpasses and transforms its limits. Perdita dances like a wave of the sea, her very body an eloquent discourse. At the opening of *The Tempest*, the alarmed comments of the Milanese noblemen on the storm-tossed ship are an instance of superfluous speech, a language at odds with direct physical action:

Antonio　　Where is the master, boson?
Boatswain　Do you not hear him? You mar our labour; keep your cabins; you do assist the storm.

Gonzalo	Nay, good, be patient.
Boatswain	When the sea is. Hence! What cares these roarers for the name of king? To cabin! silence! Trouble us not.
Gonzalo	Good, yet remember whom thou hast aboard.
Boatswain	None that I more love than myself. You are a counsellor; if you can command these elements to silence, and work the peace of the present, we will not hand a rope more.

(I.i.)

Language itself is impotent to subdue the storm, and Nature is careless of names; the sailors strive to master Nature by material labour, impatient with their passengers' idle talk. But the whole of this scene, as we shift to the next one, is suddenly revealed as the product of Prospero's magic art – of that creative word which is indeed capable of physically transforming Nature. The name of Prospero's language is Ariel, who symbolizes his word in action, the precise, fluent fulfilment of his desires. Ariel is in himself nothing, an illusion, just as language is when it becomes divorced from the material body; but because he operates as an extension of Prospero's body he takes on a definite material form. Like any other human being, Prospero is bound by physical limit and vulnerable to sensuous compassion; but through his creative word, Ariel, he is also able to transgress those bounds and be, like language, omnipresent. Through Ariel, his speech has the power, sureness and immediacy of physical action, unlike that of the storm-wracked courtiers. This ubiquity of the body as language is implicitly opposed to the fixed, appetitive body of possessive individualism, and no doubt relates to the Elizabethan myth of the king's body as eucharistically omnipresent, parcelled out among his subjects yet miraculously entire. For the body to take on the universal availability of a language, and for language to become a kind of physical gesture, is to heal the cleavage between signs and things, created and inherent values, freedom and bondage.

This harmonization of the body and language is not, however, complete. Ariel chafes under his master's control, desiring a liberty which would ironically reduce him to nothingness, disperse him into thin air. Only by being bounded is his freedom something rather than nothing. He is also a closet aesthete who wishes to sport rather than labour, manipulate reality for his own frivolous or mischievous ends rather than submit to being the executive agent of Prospero's carefully calculated strategies. Language always threatens to get out of hand and become autonomous, and Prospero has his job cut out for him in constraining Ariel to concrete material purposes. The instruments which Nature creates for its own creative alteration can always take on an independent life of their own, sever themselves from their natural root.

If Ariel needs to be tied down to the life of the body, the creaturely Caliban needs to be cranked up to the level of language. Ariel and Caliban symbolize, respectively, pure language and pure body, a freedom which threatens to transgress all restraint and a sensuous enslavement to material limit. Prospero strives to bring both of them within that dialectic of activity and passivity, bondage and transcendence, which for Shakespeare is prototypically human. In this he achieves a success rate of 50 per cent, which, as Samuel Beckett said of one of the two Calvary thieves being saved, is a reasonable percentage. For Caliban learns language only to turn it against itself, rewarding his master's efforts with curses. The developed consciousness opened for him by discourse simply thrusts him into deeper self-enslavement, inducing him to overreach his limits by attempting to murder his lord. Like alcohol, language inflates the mind but strikes the body impotent: 'here is that which will give you language, cat', says Stephano, pouring drink into Caliban's mouth.

The play's central fusion of body and language, as usual with Shakespeare, is marriage. Both Ferdinand and

Miranda find liberty within limitation: Ferdinand regards the prison of the island as 'space enough' because of her, and the modest Miranda has no ambition to see a better man than him. In sexual communion, the body itself becomes communicative discourse; and if Prospero is insistent that this interpersonal communion should be publicly institutionalized, it is less because the play dislikes fornication (though it does) than because such relationship is its sole proleptic symbol of a broader political unity. It is not easy, however, to see how you can run a political state on the lines of a marriage bed, or precisely what purchase the brave new world of the young couple has on, say, problems of economic inflation. At this point, therefore, *The Tempest* conveniently folds itself up by inviting the audience to applaud, thus breaking the magic spell by foregrounding the theatrical fictionality of its own devices. What it fails to draw attention to is the glaring contradiction on which its whole discourse effectively founders: the fact that this 'organic' restoration of a traditional social order founded upon Nature and the body rests not only on a flagrant mystification of Nature, gratuitous magical device and oppressive patriarchalism, but is actually set in the context of the very colonialism which signals the imminent victory of the exploitative, 'inorganic' mercantile bourgeoise.[2] Unable to tidy up this minor discrepancy, Shakespeare returns to the natural environment of Warwickshire with a considerable amount of money. In this, at least, he had the best of both worlds.

Conclusion

Shakespeare's utopian solution to the conflicts which beset him – an organic unity of body and language – is by definition unattainable. For the body can never be fully present in discourse: it is part of the very nature of a sign to 'absent' its referent. The symbol, as Jacques Lacan once remarked, is the death of the thing. In language we deal with the world at the level of signification, not with material objects themselves. In this sense, the estrangement of sign from thing which plagues much of Shakespeare's drama is structurally essential for the sign to function at all, and the plays are shrewdly conscious of this truth. Lacan also writes enigmatically that 'language is what hollows being into desire': because it works by difference, metonymy, a perpetual play of presence and absence, language divides and diffuses whatever lies in its path. A 'linguistic body' would thus seem something of a contradiction in terms: the solid, unified entity we call a body is fissured, rendered non-identical with itself, by the language which is its very breath.

Language, and the history of which it is the medium, extends and transforms the body's limits, as is obvious enough in the history of technology. As we have seen in the case of *King Lear*, it is this capacity to transgress or go beyond which is the very mark of human creativity, the reason why we have history rather than just biology. But as signs come to surpass the body they also threaten to escape its sensuous control, dissevering themselves from the material world and dominating that which they are meant to serve. The clearest example of this process is perhaps what Marx in *Capital* termed the 'fetishism of commodities', in which human products under capitalism, once alienated from the control of their producers, begin to set up relations between themselves which powerfully determine the social relations between men and women. Think of the stock exchange, in which interactions between stocks and shares, the signs of the accumulated labour of individuals, may result in mass unemployment.

When Shakespeare thinks of the human body, he often tends to view it as a kind of symbol of the traditional feudal social order. For that order is founded on ties of physical kinship, the sacredness of the king's physical presence, and forms of labour and social relations which are less 'abstract', than those of capitalist production. The typical economic product of feudalism, for example, is less abstract than that of capitalism because it is not a commodity on the market. A commodity is any object equally exchangeable with any other which embodies the same quantity of labour power; and what is decisive here is exchange value, rather than, as with feudalism, the actual use value of the particular product itself. In feudalism, the body also denotes the collective body politic, suitably hierarchial yet organically unified. From this viewpoint, the ceaselessly transgressive force of language comes to figure as a sign of the 'new men', the mercantilists, entrepreneurs and projectors who together form the emergent bougeoisie of Shakespeare's England. The bourgeoisie, as Marx points out in the *Communist Manifesto*, is a restlessly dynamic class, compelled by the very nature of its economic practice towards a constant thrusting-back of frontiers and blurring of traditional boundaries in its endless drive for capital accumulation. Such limitless overreaching is not a question of individual greed but is structural to the capitalist economy: in capitalist society, as in Alice's Wonderland, you have to run very fast just to stay on the spot where you

Conclusion 99

are, since any capitalist who fails to extend and transform his productive resources will rapidly go to the wall. This bourgeois social order is thus in fundamental contradiction with the older regime symbolized for Shakespeare by the physical body. But to imagine a protean language coupled to a controlling body, as with Ariel and Prospero, is among other things to allegorize a fruitful reconcilation between capitalism and feudalism. Perhaps there is a form of language which creatively exceeds the body while remaining closely moulded to its sensuous needs. Perhaps there is a way of harnessing what is most productive about bourgeois transgression to the older polity, grafting upon that settled structure certain fertile strains of dynamic energy and individual self-development.

If this is what Shakespeare has in mind, then the bad news we have to break to him, in privileged historical retrospect, is that it is an illusion. Indeed, he may well have suspected as much himself, since, as we have seen, the resolution in question is effected in the last plays only by the factitious power of magic and a ridiculously sanguine ideology of Nature. Feudalism and capitalism did not, of course, prove amenable to judicious synthesis; indeed, the latter violently uprooted the former and within a few brief centuries expunged most of its traces from the face of English society. The structural discrepancy of sign and thing became, historically, the mutual antagonism of two different modes of material production.

If the conflict of body and language in Shakespeare can be read as an allegory of class struggle, it is an allegory whose terms can be to a certain extent reversed. For from one standpoint what characterizes the emergent bourgeoisie is an intense preoccupation with the body, and what marks the traditional order is a kind of excess. Throughout the period of Shakespeare and later, the human body is being redefined as an assemblage of brute material appetites or fixed, self-interested drives; and this image of the body – Iago's, for example – belongs with an emergent bourgeois materialism deeply at odds with traditional notions of physical life. The body for Shakespeare is not this crude biological datum but an inseparable unity of fact and value: to be a human body, biologically speaking, is also to be constrained to behave in certain culturally and ethically sanctioned ways, to feel one's flesh and blood inscribed by a set of discursive norms. Bourgeois naturalism or materialism ruthlessly reduces this complex unity, dividing off facts into dead matter and values into hollow pieties to be pragmatically exploited. *Macbeth*, for example, is much preoccupied with the various meanings of 'man': the term can be zoologically descriptive, as when Macbeth tells his hired killers that they are men as far as the 'catalogue' goes; or it can make an appeal to inherent value. Macduff, whose family is slaughtered by Macbeth, is advised by Malcolm to 'Dispute it like a man', to which his swift riposte is: 'I shall do so; But I must also feel it like a man.' Malcolm's 'man' is the patriarchal stereotype of courage and emotional control; Macduff himself appeals beyond this ideology of gender to the common humanity which cuts below it, the level of shared compassion where differences of gender are not finally very important.

If a certain ideology of the body lies on the side of the bourgeoisie, there are, conversely, forms of surplus or excess which seem to belong to traditional society. The feudal economy is characterized by a certain surplus product, as must be any economy capable of reproducing itself; but this has not yet become the surplus *value* of capitalist production, which is a considerably more abstract affair. Surplus value is part of the whole circuit of exchange values under capitalism, whereas the feudal surplus can be idealized as the kind of largesse or superabundance of Nature which Shakespeare depicts in his last work. The contradictions which the drama then sets out to resolve are as follows. From the viewpoint of this traditional superabundance, imaged in Lear's 'reason not the need' or Cordelia's clemency, bourgeois exchange values appear inhumanly exact and utilitarian; yet on the other hand, exchange value itself generates a constant transgression which may be unfavourably contrasted with the settled 'measure' and reciprocity of the older regime. The complexity of Shakespeare's ideological dilemmas, that is to say, arises from the fact that they do not take the form of 'simple' contradictions, in which each term is the polar opposite of the other; on the contrary, in 'deconstructive' fashion, each term seems confusingly to inhere in its antagonist. This is obvious enough if we consider for a moment the contradictory nature of exchange value. This is a matter of precise equivalences, and so would seem to lay the basis for a kind of social order free of subjective whimsy or anarchic appetite. Yet, as we have seen often enough throughout this study, exchange value itself breeds a sort of universal chaos in which any phenomenon may be indifferently mutated into any other. 'Equivalence' is uncomfortably close to 'equivocation'. The very principle of structural regularity would thus appear to contain its own insidious undoing; the very bond between individuals, as Marx recognized in his comments on *Timon of Athens*, becomes the sword which divides them:

> If *money* is the bond binding me to *human* life, binding society to me, connecting me with nature and man, is not money the bond of all *bonds*? Can it not dissolve and bind all ties? Is it not, therefore, also the universal *agent of separation*? It is the *coin* that really *separates* as well as the real *binding agent* – the chemical power of society.
>
> Shakespeare stresses especially two properties of money:
> (1) It is the visible divinity – the transformation of all human and natural properties into their contraries, the universal confounding and distorting of things: impossibilities are soldered together by it.
> (2) It is the common whore, the common procurer of people and nations.[1]

We shall return to Marx's second point in a moment. Meanwhile we can note that, confronting with this universal confounding of things, it is possible for Shakespeare to turn back to a more traditional concept of reciprocities, that of feudalism itself. The problem, however, is not only that it is not entirely clear how such traditional mutualities escape the 'inhuman' precision of bourgeois exchange; it is also that in erasing what is destructive about capitalist surplus you also risk extirpating what is creative about it. Morover, feudal order is itself marked by a surplus which, as in *Antony and Cleopatra*, is ambivalently creative and destructive. How do you hold to a concept of measure which avoids excessive rigour, and to a concept of superfluity which avoids excessive freedom? How do you respect necessarily abstract equivalences, the very foundation of justice and social stability, while escaping a condition of universal reification; and how do you nurture a fertile surpassing of that measure without landing yourself either in the self-destructive lavishness of the old order or the anarchy of capitalist production? These antinomies may be thought through as the respective claims of justice and mercy, inherent and conferred value, law and humanity, art and Nature, or indeed as the semiotic riddle of an ideal language, at once metaphorically transformative and sensuously precise.

Samuel Johnson remarked that a quibble was Shakespeare's fatal 'Cleopatra', a beguiling coquette which seduced him from the true path of reason; and the comment goes hand in hand with Marx's description of money as the 'common whore'. Desire, as we have seen throughout this book, is for Shakespeare a dangerously destabilizing force, permutating bodies indifferently and disrupting all secure identity. It is therefore impossible for Shakespeare to project his shadowy utopia in the last comedies without drastically desexualizing the woman. In the shift from mistress to daughter, Ophelia and Desdemona to Perdita and Miranda, erotic desire is precariously sublimated, apart from the odd incestuous twinge. The woman is endowed with a degree of active power, but it is now salvific rather than sexual. Since the father–daughter relationship is 'natural', male ownership of the ¦woman may be 'organically' rather than libidinally exerted, and women thus become men's *inalienable* property. The daughter may be temporarily lost, as with Cordelia, Perdita or Marina in *Pericles*; but this loss is merely a prelude to her eventual recuperation. The woman-daughter is she who will always return, as opposed to the woman-mistress, who always may not. For the father to submit humbly to the blessing of his female child not only refurbishes an otherwise stiff-necked patriarchy with a much-needed dash of 'feminine' mildness, but provides a kind of 'natural' alternative to the fetishism of commodities. The child, product of the father and signified of his signifier, assumes a relative autonomy over him, but one of a beneficent kind. As with Lear and Cordelia, moreover, this inversion is in no sense a transformation, since the daughter manifests her filial duty in the very act of healing the patriarch.[2]

It is worth noting, finally, that 'inflation' for Shakespeare was by no means just a metaphor. Prices in England rose five times between 1530 and 1640; by the 1550s, after a century or more of relative price stability, agricultural prices were 95 per cent above those of the 1530s, and two-and-a-half times higher than prices forty years before. Industrial prices in the 1550s rose by some 70 per cent over their level in the 1530s. The 1590s witnessed some enormous price fluctuations, and the average level of agricultural prices rose by one-third.[3] The era of Shakespeare's dramatic production was rife with intense anxiety over a radically destabilized economy, and ridden with speculation about its causes. The debasement of the coinage, in the sense of the deterioration of the precious metal content of money, was widely held to be responsible for the mid-sixteenth-century financial crisis. Since food and fuel prices rose more sharply than those of other commodities, the result was a 'savage depression of the living standards of the lower half of the population. . . . The mass of [them] was forced down to a diet of black bread.'[4] These were the real material conditions endured by a great many of Shakespeare's fellow countrypeople, while Hamlet was sliding the signifier, Timon slinging around his gold, and Antony and Cleopatra savouring the fleshpots. It was not Lear's 'superflux' which was shaken to the exploited and dispossessed, but the burden of a class society in crisis. To that extent, there is an identity between Shakespeare's period and our own; the difference is that the exploited and dispossessed have now become an historical force to be reckoned with.

Notes

Chapter 1 Language: *Macbeth, Richard II, Henry IV*

For some of the theoretical writing lying behind this chapter, see Julia Kristeva, *Revolution in Poetic Language* (New York, 1984); Michel Foucault, *The Order of Things* (London, 1970); Karl Marx, Capital, vol. 1, part 1; Ernest Mandel, *Marxist Economic Theory* (London, 1962), esp. chapter 2; and Jean-Joseph Goux, 'Marx et l'inscription du travail', in *Tel Quel: Théorie d'ensemble* (Paris, 1968).

1 See Julia Kristeva, 'Women's Time', *Signs* 7:1 (1981).
2 See Stuart Clark, 'Inversion, misrule and the meaning of witchcraft', *Past and Present* 87 (1980); and Peter Stallybrass, '*Macbeth* and witchcraft', in John Russell Brown (ed.), *Focus on 'Macbeth'* (London, 1982).
3 Marx and Engels, *Selected Works* (London, 1968), p. 38. For an exhilarating discussion of these historical tendencies in relation to cultural modernism, see Marshall Berman, *All That Is Solid Melts Into Air* (London, 1983).
4 See Umberto Eco, *A Theory of Semiotics* (London, 1977), p. 7.
5 In capitalist society the use value of an object – its practical utility in fulfilling human needs – is subordinated to its exchange value, which is expressed in its price. All objects which contain the same quantity of labour can exchange with one another equally, regardless of their different uses and material qualities, and such objects are known as commodities. We shall see later how, for Shakespeare, such 'commodification' drastically affects the nature of language, sexuality and human relationships.
6 The 'imaginary' is a technical term in psychoanalytical theory to denote that narcissistic state, typical of early childhood but influencing all adult life, in which external reality seems merely a mirror in which the individual can harmoniously identify with an idealized self-image, in which there is as yet no fully independent

subjectivity and no firm borderline between subject and object. At
the point of Oedipal crisis and the acquisition of language, this
imaginary unity is ruptured: the child must come to acknowledge
itself as merely one 'signifier' in an impersonal structure of relations
which assigns it its allotted place. This structure of relations is known
as the 'symbolic order', in which each place or 'subject position' is
defined merely by its difference from the others, and in which,
because of the absence or removal of the desired object, the fullness of
the 'imaginary' image gives way to the 'lack' of desire.

Chapter 2 Desire: *A Midsummer Night's Dream, Twelfth Night*

For theoretical background, see Sigmund Freud, *Three Essays on the Theory
of Sexuality* (Harmondsworth, 1977); Jean Laplanche, *Life and Death in
Psychoanalysis* (Baltimore and London, 1976); Jacques Lacan, *Écrits*
(London, 1977); Julia Kristeva, *Desire in Language* (Oxford, 1980); and
Mikhail Bakhtin, *Rabelais and his World* (Cambridge, Mass. and London,
1968).

1 Jonathan Culler, *On Deconstruction* (London, 1983), p. 120.
2 'Adorno to Benjamin', in Ernst Bloch et al., *Aesthetics and Politics*
   (London, 1977), p. 123.

Chapter 3 Law: *The Merchant of Venice, Measure for Measure, Troilus and
        Cressida*

For theoretical background, see Ferdinand de Saussure, *Course in General
Linguistics* (London, 1978); V.N. Voloshinov, *Marxism and the Philosophy of
Language* (New York, 1973); Ludwig Wittgenstein, *Philosophical Investiga-
tions* (Oxford, 1953); Jacques Derrida, *Of Grammatology* (Baltimore,
1976) and *Writing and Difference* (London, 1978); and Jonathan Culler,
On Deconstruction (London, 1983).

1 See Paul de Man, *Allegories of Reading* (New Haven and London,
   1979), pp. 268ff.
2 For a modern view of this belief, see Maurice Merleau-Ponty, *The
   Phenomenology of Perception* (London, 1962), Part 1.
3 See Walter Cohen, '*The Merchant of Venice* and the possibilities of
   historical criticism', *English Literary History*, 49 (1982), for an excellent
   discussion of the 'archaic' or residual character of Shylock.
4 Karl Marx, *Grundrisse* (London, 1973), p. 162.
5 See Jonathan Dollimore, 'Transgression and surveillance in
   Measure for Measure', in Jonathan Dollimore and Alan Sinfield
   (eds), *Political Shakespeare* (Manchester, 1985), for an illuminating
   treatment of the dialectic between law and desire in the play.

Chapter 4 'Nothing': *Othello, Hamlet, Coriolanus*

For theoretical background, see Freud, 'Some Neurotic Mechanisms in Jealousy, Paranoia and Homosexuality', in *The Complete Psychological Works of Sigmund Freud*, standard edition, ed. James Strachey (London, 1953–), vol. 18; and 'Mourning and Melancholia', standard edition, vol. 14. See also Fredric Jameson, 'Imaginary and Symbolic in Lacan', in *Literature and Psychoanalysis* (Yale French Studies 55/56, 1977).

1 See E. A. M. Colman, *The Dramatic Use of Bawdy in Shakespeare* (London, 1974), pp. 15–18; and David Wilberns, 'Shakespeare's nothing', in M. Schwartz and C. Kahn (eds), *Representing Shakespeare* (Baltimore, 1980). There is some controversy over how common this sexual connotation of the word was. It would certainly seem to be present in Hamlet's crude remarks to Ophelia before 'The Mouse-trap', and possibly also in the title *Much Ado About Nothing*, which, since 'ado' can mean 'copulation', may be doubly suggestive. It need not be supposed, however, that when Lear asks Cordelia what she can say to win his favour, she replies 'female genitals, my lord'.

2 See Jacqueline Rose, 'Sexuality in the reading of Shakespeare: *Hamlet* and *Measure for Measure*', in John Drakakis (ed.), *Alternative Shakespeares* (London, 1985).

3 See Francis Barker, *The Tremulous Private Body* (London, 1984), for a suggestive treatment of *Hamlet* in this respect.

Chapter 5 Value: *King Lear, Timon of Athens, Antony and Cleopatra*

For theoretical background, see Sebastiano Timpanaro, *On Materialism* (London, 1975), chapter 1; Norman Geras, *Marx and Human Nature* (London, 1983); Terry Eagleton, 'Nature and Violence: the Prefaces of Edward Bond', in *Critical Quarterly*, vol. 26, nos 1 & 2 (spring and summer 1984); and Gilles Deleuze, *Nietzsche and Philosophy* (London, 1983).

1 To claim that the lines are trite is one of the rare blindspots of Franco Moretti's *Signs Taken As Wonders* (London, 1983), the second chapter of which is a strikingly original essay on Elizabethan and Jacobean tragedy.

Chapter 6 Nature: *As You Like It, The Winter's Tale, The Tempest*

For theoretical background, see Raymond Williams, *The Country and the City* (London, 1973), and *Problems in Materialism and Culture* (London, 1980), Part 3.

1 For one of the most penetrating treatments of *As You Like It*, and of Shakespeare in general, see Malcolm Evans, *Signifying Nothing* (forthcoming).

2 See Paul Brown, ' "This thing of darkness I acknowledge mine": *The Tempest* and the discourse of colonialism', in J. Dollimore and A. Sinfield (eds), *Political Shakespeare* (Manchester, 1985); and Francis Barker and Peter Hulme, 'Nymphs and reapers heavily vanish: the discursive con-texts of *The Tempest*', in John Drakakis (ed.), *Alternative Shakespeares* (London, 1985).

Conclusion

For theoretical background, see Paul Sweezy et al., *The Transition from Feudalism to Capitalism* (London, 1978); Perry Anderson, *Lineages of the Absolutist State* (London, 1974); and C. B. Macpherson, *The Political Theory of Possessive Individualism* (Oxford, 1962).

1 *Marx and Engels on Literature and Art* (Moscow, 1976), p. 137.

2 For feminist criticism of Shakespeare, see Juliet Dusinberre, *Shakespeare and the Nature of Women* (London, 1975); G. Greene et al. (eds), *The Woman's Part: Feminist Criticism of Shakespeare* (Urbana, 1980); Simon Shepherd, *Amazons and Warrior Women: Varieties of Feminism in Seventeenth-Century Drama* (Brighton, 1981); Marilyn French, *Shakespeare's Division of Experience* (London, 1982); and Lisa Jardine, *Still Harping on Daughters: Women and Drama in the Age of Shakespeare* (Brighton, 1983).

3 See R. B. Outhwaite, *Inflation in Tudor and Early Stuart England* (London, 1969).

4 Christopher Hill, *Reformation to Industrial Revolution* (Harmondsworth, 1969), p. 83.

Index

Nerissa (in *The Merchant of Venice*),
    40
Nietzsche, 85, 86
Northumberland, Earl of (in
    Richard II), 12
Northumberland, Earl of (in *Henry
    IV*), 16, 17
'nothing', 64–75
    death as, 12
    meaning female genitals, 64–6,
        107

Oberon (in *A Midsummer Night's
    Dream*), 22, 23, 25, 31
Octavius (in *Antony and Cleopatra*),
    88
Olivia (in *Twelfth Night*), 32, 33, 34
Ophelia (in *Hamlet*), 74, 102, 107
Orlando (in *As You Like It*), 90
Orsino (in *Twelfth Night*), 26, 33,
    34
Oswald (in *King Lear*), 83
Othello (in *Othello*), 64–71
Othello, 64–70, 71, 72, 80, 99, 102
Outhwaite, R. B., 108

Pandarus (in *Troilus and Cressida*),
    60
paranoia, 65, 67, 77
patriarchy, 6, 21, 22, 65, 68, 96,
    100, 103
Patroclus (in *Troilus and Cressida*),
    23, 61
Perdita (in *The Winter's Tale*), 91,
    92, 93, 102, 103
Pericles, 103
Pinter, Harold: *The Birthday Party*,
    30
political stability *see* social order
Polixenes (in *The Winter's Tale*), 91
Polonius (in *Hamlet*), 73
Portia (in *The Merchant of Venice*),
    36–42, 45, 47
Prince Hal *see* Hal, Prince
Prospero (in *The Tempest*), 94, 95,
    96, 99

Proust, 65
Provost (in *Measure for Measure*), 13
Prufrock, J. Alfred, 72
Puck (in *A Midsummer Night's
    Dream*), 24, 25, 26
puns, 1, 2, 10, 17, 31, 32, 34

Regan (in *King Lear*), 76, 77, 80, 82
Richard II (in *Richard II*), 9, 10,
    11, 12
Richard II, 9–15
Rosalind (in *As You Like It*), 11, 90
Rose, Jacqueline, 107
Rosencrantz and Guildenstern (in
    Hamlet), 72
Ross (in *Macbeth*), 4

self, 15, 23–4, 61–2, 72
    as currency for social barter, 24
    truth to, 73, 80, 81
sexual desire *see* desire
Shakespeare
    and actor's role, 13
    as conservative patriarch, x
    and desire, 18, 20, 24, 102
    and human nature, 45, 95, 100
    and ideology, 101
    and language, 58, 69, 97
    and marriage, 21
    and nature, 89, 90, 93
    and social order, 1, 7, 74, 98, 99
    textual productivity in, 5
    villains in, 4, 73
    see also titles of plays
Shepherd, Simon, 108
Shylock (in *The Merchant of Venice*),
    36–47, 106
Sinfield, Alan, 106, 108
social order, 1, 7, 11, 15, 16, 17, 20,
    39, 47–8, 57, 74, 87, 93, 98, 99
Stallybrass, Peter, 105
surplus, 81–2, 87, 88, 100, 104
    in Nature, 93, 100
Sweezy, Paul, 108

The Tempest, 8, 93–6, 99, 102

Index by Hannah Cole